ecological literary criticism

ecological literary criticism

Romantic Imagining and the Biology of Mind

karl kroeber

Columbia University Press

New York

Columbia University Press
New York   Chichester, West Sussex
Copyright © 1994 Columbia University Press

Library of Congress Cataloging-in-Publication Data
Kroeber, Karl, 1926–
Ecological literary criticism : romantic imagining and the biology of mind /
Karl Kroeber.
p. cm.
Includes bibliographical references and index.
ISBN 0–231–10028–0
ISBN 0–231–10029–9 (pbk.)
1. Romanticism. 2. Criticism. 3. Ecology in literature.
I. Title.
PN56.R7K76   1994
801'.95' 09045—dc20   94–5232
                                                        C IP

Printed in the United States of America

c 10 9 8 7 6 5 4 3 2 1
p 10 9 8 7 6 5 4 3 2 1

This book is gratefully dedicated to the critics with whom during the past four decades I have disagreed, some of whom I cite in the following pages: without the stimulus of their contrariety I would have accomplished nothing.

Opposition is true Friendship.

contents

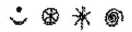

ecological literary criticism

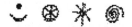

Introducing Ecological Criticism

My purpose in this book is to encourage the development of an ecologically oriented literary criticism. This criticism, escaping from the esoteric abstractness that afflicts current theorizing about literature, seizes opportunities offered by recent biological research to make humanistic studies more socially responsible. Biologists have arrived at the frontier of revolutionary new conceptions of humanity's place within the natural world. Humanists willing to think beyond self-imposed political and metaphysical limits of contemporary critical discourse can use these scientific advances to make literary studies contribute to the practical resolution of social and political conflicts that rend our society. Humanists could help to ensure, for example, that the effects on our world of new biological research are beneficent rather than malign.

Ecological literary criticism concentrates on linkages between natural and cultural processes. It thus functions transmissively. Instead of withdrawing the objects of its study into a hermetic discourse, it seeks to enhance widespread appreciation of how literary art may connect cultural experiences to natural facts. Ecological criticism is holistic, which requires that its primary focus be directed to the individuality of works of art—and of the audiences responding to them. Ecological criticism can therefore foster a cosmopolitan appreciation of differences and uniquenesses, especially in the processes of cultural transformation. It takes a form distinct from the "philosophic" essay currently popular with critics, tending toward narrative structures more responsive to the singularity of historical phenomena. Not seeking supposedly universal principles, and concentrating on contingencies of cultural history, ecological criticism resists current academic overemphasis on the rationalistic at the expense of sensory, emotional, and imaginative aspects of art.

I will outline the essential features of this critical mode by reassessing British romantic poetry of the early nineteenth century, the first literature to anticipate contemporary biological conceptions. Romantic poems came into being with the emergence of "modern" culture and have often been used to articulate twentieth-century principles of criticism. Romantic poetry thus dramatizes with peculiar clarity both why ecological thinking has been slow to penetrate literary criticism and why it is especially needed today.

I align myself with Jonathan Bate's definition of an ecological approach as antagonistic to recent academic criticism of romantic poetry.[1] I share Bate's view that romantic "nature poetry" is neither apolitical nor a disguise for covert ideological polemics. Poetry about nature expresses the romantic poets' deepest political commitments, the profundity of which, ironically, has been obscured by "new historicists" dismissing romantic descriptions of nature as mere "displacements" of unconscious political motives. This approach falsifies the romantics' most intense, original, and enduringly significant discoveries of humanity's place in the natural world. Contrastively misleading are "rhetorical formalists" who preceded the new historicists, notably those of the "Yale School." Contrary to the claims of these enthusiasts of "the sublime," romantic poets at their best thought and wrote in the tradition of what Alan Bewell has called "environmental historicism," and were neither seekers after an unattainable transcendence nor anxiety-ridden prophets of nihilism but rather forerunners of a new biological, materialistic understanding of humanity's place in the natural cosmos.[2]

The deficiencies of both sets of critics are the reverse of their virtues, their revelations of partial truths of substantial value. The partial truth emphasized by the Yale rhetorical critics is that romantic responses to nature were intensely interactive, requiring the poets to question the function of consciousness in a world of natural processes. The work of these critics has heightened our awareness of the complex self-interrogations

fundamental to the best romantic poetry. Tilottima Rajan's recent study of Shelley in *The Supplement of Reading* superbly exemplifies how intelligently developed deconstructive readings of romantic poets may enhance our appreciation of why their poetry was linguistically so innovative.[3]

The partial truth displayed by the new historicists is the romantic poets' pervasive sense of responsibility, how the simple and attractive surface of their verse often conceals the tortuousness of their social questionings. These critics usefully fasten attention on how the intricacy of immediate historical context determines the very particular fashion in which each poem came into being. Illustrative is a recent essay by Paul Magnuson demonstrating how Coleridge's lyric "Frost and Midnight" was shaped by the poet's specific political engagements at the time of its original publication.[4]

The defective partialness of both approaches springs from their common rootedness in a Cold War mind-set.[5] Both "schools" reflect fundamental attitudes of superpower oppositionalism deriving from the global political situation produced by World War II. Both schools favor violent, even apocalyptic rhetoric based on the condemnation of ideological "enemies," usually no more specifically identified than the "communists" Senator McCarthy attacked or the "capitalists" excoriated by Soviet Marxists. This ideological oppositionalism tends to conceive of science in terms of technological power and to ignore less dramatic developments in the understanding of normal biological processes of continuity and interconnection. These, however, were the phenomena that fascinated the romantic poets (as they do modern biologists), the poets being less concerned with transcending natural existence than with transfiguring it. "Science" for Cold War critics is represented as a mere agency of absolute power, without historical complexities of self-contradiction.

The romantic focus on transfiguring rather than transcending biased them toward narrative modes of poetry. That preference has been concealed even by the *form* of commentaries favored by both new historicists and Yale rhetoricians. Marjorie Levinson, for example, has written a book about Wordsworth in which she discusses only three lyric poems and "Michael," which she treats as a "lyricized narrative." Analogously, Paul de Man analyzed Shelley's "Triumph of Life" in a celebrated essay that totally obscured the poem's undergirding narrative structure.[6] Cold War critics under the spell of antagonistic oppositionalism, and conceiving

3

relationships exclusively in terms of power struggles, tend to treat all poems as lyricized representations of "primal scenes," that is, as schematic dramatizations of universal psychic conflicts.

Not only did the romantics write an enormous number of narrative poems but (contrary to Levinson's claims) they consistently narrativized their lyrics, using stories to give shape to their lyricism, as Wordsworth does in "Tintern Abbey," as Shelley does in "Hymn to Intellectual Beauty," as Coleridge does in "This Lime Tree Bower," as Keats does in "Ode to a Nightingale," and as Byron does in his last love poem addressed to his Greek servant boy, Loukas Chalandritasnos, which I quote complete to emphasize how easily romantic poets turn to story as an appropriate form for representing intense emotion.

> I watched thee when the foe was at our side
>   Ready to strike at him—or thee and me,
> Were safety hopeless—rather than divide
>   Aught with one loved save love and liberty.
>
> I watched thee on the breakers, when the rock
>   Received our prow and all was storm and fear,
> And bade thee cling to me through every shock;
>   This arm would be thy bark, or breast thy bier.
>
> I watched thee when the fever glazed thine eyes,
>   Yielding my couch and stretched me on the ground,
> When overworn with watching, ne'er to rise
>   From thence if thou an early grave hadst found.
>
> The earthquake came, and rocked the quivering wall,
>   And men and nature reeled as if with wine.
> Whom did I seek around the tottering hall?
>   For thee. Whose safety first provide for? Thine.
>
> And when convulsive throes denied my breath
>   The faintest utterance to my fading thought,
> To thee—to thee—e'en in the gasp of death
>   My spirit turned, oh! oftner than it ought.

> Thus much and more; and yet thou lov'st me not,
> And never wilt! Love dwells not in our will,
> Nor can I blame thee, though it be my lot
> To strongly, wrongly, vainly love thee still.[7]

This painfully personal lyric consists of an accurate historical account of the physical experiences Byron and his servant underwent in the course of the poet's labors for Greek revolutionaries. Such *narrative* factuality highlights Byron's pitiless awareness of the futility of his passion, endowing his homoeroticism with characteristic romantic qualities: intensity of extended (not merely instantaneous) experience, experience unabashedly subjectivized and rooted (whatever its dark flowering) in sensations of pleasure, and simultaneously focusing the complex play upon the poet of intricately specific sociopolitical pressures.

What the successes of late twentieth-century critics have disastrously obscured is the British romantic poets' extraordinary emphasis on *pleasure* as the foundation of poetry, even political verse.[8] Because the ideological-philosophic commitments of Cold War critics lead them to subordinate everything to "the will for power," they give little attention to the potency of delights treasured by romantics. These poets tended to regard thought as constituted of emotions. Wordsworth, for example, calls thoughts "representatives of all our past feelings." So pleasurable feelings—obviously— should be the basis of creative, exuberant, constructive thinking. Yet the romantics' high valuation of pleasurable experience seldom lured them into evading the truth that humankind's special capacity for joy makes us simultaneously vulnerable to excruciating suffering. The most powerful and enduring romantic poems, therefore, culminate in contradiction (as in Byron's last lyric) or ambivalence. For the romantics, the highest human attainment is to achieve and sustain intensely contradictory feelings.

The primacy that the romantics gave to enjoyment with a resulting aspiration to (*not* the wish to escape from) ambivalence is ignored by Cold War critics, not only because of their preoccupation with power but also because they assume that all societies alienate mankind from nature. The romantics, in contrast, made pleasure fundamental to human accomplishments because they believed that humankind *belonged* in, could and should be at home within, the world of natural processes. This is the foundation of what I shall call their proto-ecological views.[9] These views are comprehensible (indeed, discernible) only if we suspend current presuppositions about humankind's inescapable discomfort within its natural habitat and the inevitability of mankind's self-defining antagonism to nature.

The moment is propitious for revising these assumptions, because in the past decade and a half the flourishing of another mode of literary criticism—feminism—has encouraged cooperation between humanistic and scientific research, at the same time offering valuable techniques for interrogating every kind of will-to-power criticism. However intricate and unstable present (and future) relations between feminist and ecological criticism may be, their underlying tendencies run toward mutual reinforcement. Leaving other aspects of this relation until later, I shall here take time only to suggest how one major strand of feminist thinking supports—indeed, is essential to—ecological criticism's central purpose.

Beginning from a perception that the current Western concept of individuality is in fact a concept of *male* individuality, Jessica Benjamin argues that "the principle of rationality which social theorists since Weber have seen as the hallmark of modernity—the rationality that reduces the social world to objects of exchange, calculation, and control—is in fact a male rationality."[10] This means that not only leftist rationality but even seemingly apolitical scientific work must be scrutinized severely. Ecologically oriented sciences themselves, however, encourage the critiques of "male rationality" that Benjamin advocates, because ecologically oriented sciences, as I shall demonstrate, came into being in response to the explanatory shortcomings of the modernistic "principle of rationality." Critical work such as Benjamin's suggests how an ecological criticism must inevitably solidify the changes in conventional conceptions of the relation between humanism and the natural sciences that is implicitly demanded by much of the best feminist scholarship.

Benjamin, for example, develops her critique of the dominance of modernist male rationality in this fashion:

> The psychic repudiation of femininity, which includes the negation of dependency and mutual recognition, is homologous with the social banishment of nurturance and intersubjective relatedness to the private domestic world of women and children. . . . As the principle of pure self-assertion comes to govern the public world of men, human agency is

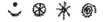

enslaved by the objects it produces, deprived of the personal authorship and recognizing response that are essential to subjectivity. . . . The subordination of all aspects of life to the instrumental principles of the public world also subverts the very values of private life, and thus threatens the maternal aspects of recognition: nurturance (the recognition of need), and attunement (the recognition of feelings).[11]

These phenomena are, of course, the result of attitudes that fully triumphed in Western civilization only in the nineteenth century, reaching their apogee perhaps in the first half of this century. It was the impending tyranny of such thinking (and of the social structures it produced) that the romantic poets resisted. What I call their proto-ecological views were marshaled to assert the value of feeling, particularly pleasurable feeling, individualized imaginative subjectivity, and awareness of human interdependencies against the rationalized pseudoimpersonality encouraged by industrialized imperialism (with its accompanying "reformist" utopianism) emerging in their epoch. Romantic assertions, therefore, often take the form of defenses of what we now recognize as a "feminine" perspective, most significantly in representations of "feminine" components in masculine individualities, as Wordsworth does, for example, in "Tintern Abbey," and as Keats does in his "Ode to Psyche."[12] The self-critical components in romantic celebrations of individuality are, in fact, usually directed against what we now identify as masculinist conceptions of individualism.

Today's developing ecological orientation of biological and chemical research has carried this portion of a "male-oriented" science very far toward a "feminist" understanding of nature—emphatically not a vision of nature simply as female, not as an object laying itself open to exploitation, to rape. Contemporary biological thinking, as is illustrated in the Neural Darwinism I sketch in my final chapter, no longer identifies individuality with autonomy and separation. For leading contemporary biologists, the individuality of an organism is not definable except through its interactions with its environment, through its interdependencies. An organism's uniqueness consists in "intersubjective" connections and is determined not by separation but by "attunement," participation in "communities" (both inside itself and in the external environment) defined by historically individualized mutualities of need and desire. It is no accident that women like Ellen Swallow and Barbara McClintock have contributed so significantly to ecological thinking, which seems every year more hospitable to the new "dynamic" scientific objectivity proposed by Evelyn Keller, one that "actively draws on the commonality between mind and nature" and stresses "attunement and similarity between knower and known."[13]

One way to assure the continuing influence of such rethinkings of fundamental presuppositions of biological science would be to develop an ecological criticism. Such criticism's basic assumptions and commitments—above all, its attempt to bring back into communication scientific and humanistic research—are entirely in accord with the radical reenvisioning of humankind's natural condition that is the driving force in some of today's most valuable feminist scholarship.[14]

However much the romantic poets anticipated views for us more cogently articulated by current feminists, the poets' innovativeness had to be given shape within the contours of the scientific conceptions of their day. The direction of the poets' thought was toward a biologically materialistic understanding of the human mind. Sciences such as chemistry, biology, and physiology, however, were insufficiently developed then to give much support to such conceptions of mental processes. This is one reason it was difficult for the poets to sustain their faith in pleasure, to continue welcoming the experiences of natural life without retreating to transcendental consolations or a skepticism corrosive of their idealistic faith in "the pleasure which there is in life itself," the Wordsworthian phrase from "Michael" that refers to a life of unspectacular but continuous interactivity with one's environment.

"I would believe," Wordsworth tells us in "Tintern Abbey," that there is "abundant recompense" for the losses he recognizes intrinsic to our natural maturation whose completion is death. Wordsworth here characteristically expresses hope, not certainty. Hope, not certainty, is the dominant romantic mode. Wordsworth, in fact, could not keep his naturalistic hopefulness alive as he grew older. He was not able to sustain the tensions he so grippingly dramatizes in "Michael," "The Ruined Cottage," and "The Fountain." He fell back into a conventional Christian piety that betrays his early vision. Even Shelley, who bitterly criticized that betrayal, was himself strongly tempted to retreat into a form of Platonic idealism. Self-betrayal, especially betrayal of faith in the pleasurable

potentialities of natural being, is the essential, underlying, ever-threatening antagonist to romantic optimistic idealism.

An ecological view of the world, even a proto-ecological one, must be fundamentally materialistic, since its basic premise is that human beings are appropriately situated here on earth. How nature appears to be ordered, the romantics realized, is largely shaped by our internalized cultural presuppositions. To judge these, to reinforce or revise them, we must estimate how congruent they in fact are to the materiality of the physical universe that we experience every moment of our lives. In England by the end of the eighteenth century the materiality of the natural cosmos had become a source of special interest. As agricultural civilization gave way to industrial civilization—which includes, of course, the industrializing of agriculture—the possibility of humanity's control of natural processes and the results for good or ill of such control seized the imagination of intellectuals, businessmen, engineers, wealthy landowners, financiers, politicians, and poets. The urge toward deeper understanding and mastery of the physical world was founded on the development during the preceding two hundred years of modern science emanating from the Copernican revolution. The imaginative effects of this development may be defined in terms of the two most celebrated instruments of discovery it produced. The telescope gave access to what lay beyond what everyone could see, expanding human visions of the universe as a macrosystem. The microscope gave access to what was too small for everyone to see and enlarged understanding of how the natural world was founded upon an infinity of microprocesses.

We take these instruments so much for granted that we forget how urgently they inspired not only reconceptions of what "nature" consisted but also rethinking of what man's best relation to nature might be. Such reconceivings inevitably produced growing awareness of humankind's impact on the natural world. Not only chemistry and biology began to be practiced in fashions that seem much like our idea of how best to pursue scientific study, but then, too, modern anthropology with its refinement of Vico's radical concept of culture crystallized.[15] So it should not surprise us that the politics of romantic poetry is inextricably intertwined with the poets' ideas about the physical world of nature. Whatever their personal ideological bias, all the poets repudiated "unnatural" political positions, those that they thought ran contrary

9

to natural processes, to espouse political positions they believed to be in accord with those processes.

The foregoing generalization is necessary because the political biases of the romantic poets were far more various—running from the extremely reactionary to the violently radical—as well as more complicated than recent critics admit. Their mistake derives in part from not figuring into their political equations so-called minor poetry of the epoch. Even a superficial consideration of, say, Gifford, Campbell, Scott, and Southey along with just a few of the women poets of the day (Landon, Tighe, Robinson, More, Barbauld, etc.) demolishes the simplified ideological oppositionalism that has too often determined new historicists' political summations.

Illustrative of the romantics' naturalistic orientation toward political issues is Wordsworth's sonnet "I Grieved for Buonaparte," which at first glance may seem purely political, without reference to the natural world.

> I grieved for Buonaparte, with a vain
> And an unthinking grief! The tenderest mood
> Of that Man's mind—what can it be? what food
> Fed his first hopes? what knowledge could *he* gain?
> 'T is not in battles that from youth we train
> The governor who must be wise and good,
> And temper with the sternness of the brain
> Thoughts motherly, and meek as womanhood.
> Wisdom doth live with children round her knees:
> Books, leisure, perfect freedom, and the talk
> Man holds with week-day man in the hourly walk
> Of the mind's business: these are the degrees
> By which true Sway doth mount; this is the stalk
> True Power doth grow on; and her rights are these.[16]

Most astonishing in this sonnet is how Buonaparte fades out of it. By the last lines the French ruler who shakes all of Europe is forgotten in a representation of "True Power" whose "stalk" is simple, common, "homely" social behavior, so down-to-earth as to appear entirely "natural." This appearance arises mainly not from the plant metaphor but from Wordsworth's adroit generalizing. Though he depicts social behavior and

relations, he does so in a fashion in no way limited by ideological or national peculiarities. The attitudes and ways of behaving affirmed are made to seem elemental, characteristic of *any* normal human life.[17] The "stalk" upon which "True Power" grows thus is nourished by meekness, motherliness, "with children round her knees"—a generic familial image with a strong feminine bias that makes thought of imperial pomp absurd. In this association of "True Power" with "natural" maternity, Buonaparte must disappear as simply unfitted for what is appropriate to all healthy human communities.

A decade earlier, Wordsworth, as he tells us in *The Prelude*, had hated and feared Robespierre as a perverter of revolutionary ideals. It may be that the poet had learned from the subsequent rise of Buonaparte that successful opposition to a tyrant on *his* terms may produce only a more dangerous tyrant. In any event, Wordsworth's technique with Buonaparte is not to attack him but to "dismiss" him by articulating how meaningless is his celebrity when scrutinized in the light of the unpretentious truths of "natural" human life. The French ruler is diminished to nothing not because he is ideologically evil or mistaken but because he has made himself discordant with the elemental rhythms by which humans adapt to nature's beneficence.

The key to Wordsworth's maneuver is given in the opening line, which in 1802 could only be startling. How could—or why should—an Englishman grieve for England's greatest enemy? To understand Wordsworth's point, one may think of the analogy, in our time, of Alexander Solzhenitsyn writing, "I grieved for Stalin." Like some other Englishmen, Wordsworth had favored sociopolitical principles popularized at the commencement of the French Revolution, applauding the fall of the Bastille and the overthrow of abuses of the *ancien regime*. The rise to power of Robespierre and the violence he and his followers unleashed shook and sometimes shattered that idealism. Then, after some years of war between England and France, Buonaparte gained supreme power. He threatened England with invasion and moved toward the imperialistic rule he fully seized when he crowned himself emperor. Around 1802, when "I Grieved for Buonaparte" was composed, people such as Wordsworth were forced even more seriously to reexamine their earlier idealism. Some, like Wordsworth, concluded that Robespierre and Buonaparte were not, as he had at first assumed, perverters of the true spirit of

11

the French Revolution. They were, more disturbingly, genuine expressions of inherent tendencies of the Revolution. In analogous fashion, in our century Solzhenitsyn, who began as an idealistic communist and a patriotic Soviet soldier, concluded that Lenin and Stalin were not perverters of Soviet Marxism but authentic expressors of fundamental tendencies in that ideology.

To arrive at such perceptions is deeply troubling, because they reveal that one has unwittingly supported what one despised. How could we so betray ourselves? How can our idealism so disastrously mislead us? All the significant political thinking of the romantic poets is focused by those questions. [18] But at their most effective the English romantic poets did not, like some of their Continental contemporaries and successors, seek a religious solution to the problem of ideological self-betrayal. In their finest poetry it is the natural world to which they turn in trying to understand and correct their capacity to deceive themselves and distort their profoundest idealisms.

In diverse ways and with diverse kinds of qualifications the romantic poets agreed with Wordsworth that nature and human consciousness were splendidly adapted to one another. So even Coleridge, who devoted the most extended efforts of his intellectual life to constructing justifications for traditional Christian faith, in his early "recantation" poem, "France: An Ode," finds the authentic spirit of liberty in natural processes.

> Thou speedest on thy subtle pinions,
> The guide of homeless winds, and playmate of the waves!
> And there I felt thee on that sea-cliff's verge,
> Whose pines, scarce travelled by the breeze above,
> Had made one murmur with the distant surge!
> Yes, while I stood and gazed, my temples bare,
> And shot my being through earth, sea, and air,
> Possessing all things with intensest love,
> O Liberty! my spirit felt thee there.
>
> (97–105)

Modern readers may have difficulty taking Coleridge's words as literally as he seems to have intended them. We are surprised by the bald assertion that true freedom of spirit underlying political libertarianism is to be

found by engaging ourselves with natural processes. Even the idea of being able to project one's conscious self into the natural world strikes us as incredible. Our incredulity should tell us how deeply we have internalized a conception of men and women as alienated beings. For the younger Coleridge, however, great processes of natural existence, not any one political philosophy or particular ideology, offered access to a fundamental human experience of freedom, which he thus identifies as, at root, a natural, materialistic characteristic of earthly life.

For Coleridge, *liberty* is more than an ideologically loaded word, a political slogan. Liberty is a physically experiential possibility. Against that possibility must be tested the claims of any political dogma. The experience he represents is individual participation in the uncontrollable vitality manifested in clouds, waves, and wind-swung forest branches whose energy fulfills "eternal laws."

> O ye loud Waves! and O ye Forests high!
> And O ye clouds that far above me soared!
> Thou rising sun! thou blue rejoicing Sky!
> Yea, everything that is and will be free!
>
> (1–4)[19]

Coleridge can imagine the sky as joyous because he feels that freedom of individual being is to participate fulfilling in a dynamic unity of forces vastly greater than himself but to which he can satisfyingly belong. What today we would tend to call an ecosystem for him images the essential structure of a genuinely, rather than a speciously, liberated existence.

What one might call the realistic underside of such idealistic romantic proto-ecological views was pungently articulated by Thomas Malthus. No discussion of romantic attitudes toward nature can be adequate that ignores Malthus—and the disturbance he caused his contemporaries. With good reason. He was in some ways a perfect romantic. No one more firmly demanded that any political system be tested against what we know about natural processes. Malthus argued against social utopianists, prophets of progress and the perfecting of human society, so far as they tried to contravene fundamental laws of nature.

Malthus shaped his argument by treating human societies demographically, as quantifiable "populations," laying a groundwork for Darwin's more sophisticated "population thinking," which has become commonplace nowadays. But Malthus's innovative study of populations, mankind in masses,[20] did not entirely blind him (as it did some who seized on his work for particular political ends) to the significance of his findings, especially their ethical significance, for individuals and individual behavior.[21] Malthus's work points us toward the seeming paradox central to the romantic vision of the natural world: holistic conceptions of nature necessarily lead to close attention to the individuality of the elements constituting the total system.

In our time that paradox reappears, for an obvious example, in chaos theory, which recognizes that weather prediction may be thrown off because a butterfly flaps its wings. Without our mathematics of nonlinear equations, the romantics could not do much better than turn to Spinoza. His appeal to them lay in his denying the transcendence of God. He asserted, instead, the divinity—meaning the eternal vitality, the ceaselessly self-creating character—of the natural world. As youthful Shelley puts it his note to his declaration in *Queen Mab*, "There is no God!" (7.13): "This negation must be understood solely to affect a creative Deity. The hypothesis of a pervading Spirit, coeternal with the universe, remains unshaken."[22]

The inescapable, if joyous, "determinism" intrinsic to Spinoza's system was acceptable to the romantics because it allowed individuals to be connected with the eternal vitality of the entire universe. As Coleridge's "France: An Ode" demonstrates, romantic liberty is based upon consciously projective participation in the eternal ongoingness of self-transforming natural processes. The romantic capacity to find freedom and personal fulfillment through conscious engagement with a dynamic cosmos seems difficult for many recent critics to understand. A way toward comprehension is offered, perhaps, by the poets' tendency to move away from Spinoza and toward Lamarck and ideas of evolution. The romantics understood "nature" not as static but as mutable, evanescent, and even developing. In any kind of evolutionary perspective, the life of each particular form is defined by the continuity of its interactions with its shifting environments.

The romantics' tendency toward what might be called experience environmentally conceived is important as the foundation of their resistance to aesthetic doctrines in the "art for art's sake" mode. They did not wish to remove poetry into an "aesthetic" realm. They insisted on the practical

efficacy and the practical duties of art—not just to the social but also to the natural world. Their poems repeatedly try to demonstrate that poetry cannot do well for one world without meeting its responsibilities to the other. The romantics did not always succeed, and they often were torn by doubts about their own firmest convictions. For those of us today who find ourselves struggling with difficult questions of how best to relate cultural productions to natural conditions, however, there are useful lessons in these romantic aspirings to connect nature and culture—so different from recent morose lamentations about their supposed inexorable antagonism.

Before I attempt in the following chapters to give substance and color to the foregoing outline, I want to disabuse readers of one or two misconceptions that this preparatory sketch may have aroused.

It is *not* my purpose to analyze the romantic poets' knowledge of the theoretical and practical sciences of their day. Wordsworth, Coleridge, Shelley, and Keats did possess varying degrees of detailed and accurate knowledge of the natural sciences.[23] They developed that understanding because they were interested in the natural world and what might constitute humankind's best relations to it. For my purposes, however, their scientific knowledge is germane only to the fashion in which they represent experiences of natural phenomena. I am not so concerned, to cite a specific example, with whether or not the last stanza of Keats's "Ode to Psyche" as a whole reflects what Keats learned in lectures at Guy's Hospital about the physical structure of the brain.[24] I am more interested in the fact that such lectures are a possible source, and therefore alert us to implications of several details in the stanza, such as the phrase "the wreath'd trellis of a working brain." A trellis is a framework used specifically to direct the growth of vines or climbing plants. Keats, then, represents his creative power through an image of cooperation between human intention and natural flora. That imaginative figuring, rather than the possible fidelity of Keats's reproducing the physiological knowledge of his epoch, is the focus of my interest.

The training Keats received, however, is symptomatic of the rapid development of science at the beginning of the nineteenth century, a development that encouraged the romantic poets' interest in the natural world and enhanced their concern to define through their poetry the best relations between nature and culture. An entertaining illustration of the congruence of natural science and poetry is found in John Aikin's 1777 *Essay on the Application of Natural History to Poetry*, which regards contemporary poetry as "worn down, enfeebled, and fettered" by "a perpetual repetition of the same images, clad in almost the same language," and "a real want of variety in poetic imagery, proceeding from a scarcity of original observations of nature." The source of this "insipidity of Modern Poetry" for Aikin, notably, is not literary imitativeness but "a too cursory and general survey of objects, without exploring their minuter distinctions and mutual relations," a condition "only to be rectified by accurate and attentive observation, conducted upon somewhat of a scientific plan."[25]

Aikin's little book, revealing the significant replacement in intellectual discourse of the term *natural philosophy* with *natural history* founded on material discoveries through careful observation (which I have emblematized with the microscope), admirably expresses the tone of congruence of interests between scientists and poets that was a foundation of romantic nature poetry. The poets, nevertheless, were not scientists. The poets claimed, in fact, that *they* more comprehensively and usefully discerned the proper relations of human beings to the natural cosmos. Wordsworth was explicit as to the superiority of poets to scientists, stressing, significantly, the poets' intrinsically social function: "The Man of Science seeks truth as a remote and unknown benefactor; he cherishes and loves it in his solitude: the Poet, singing a song in which all human beings join with him, rejoices in the presence of truth as our visible friend and hourly companion."[26] Later Shelley would assert that "we have more knowledge than we can digest," urging that we must learn to "imagine what we know," an education clearly to be carried out less through scientific research than humanistic learning.

It was the close attention to processes characteristic of natural phenomena that attracted romantic poets to scientific studies yet impelled them to insist on an imaginative, rather than a scientifically rationalized, understanding of the meaning of human experiences of the natural world. Science, they believed, could on occasion provide a means of increasing our ability to learn from, and more efficaciously interact with, the natural world. So the poets were ready to employ scientific knowledge in shaping their representations. In so doing, however, they confirmed

the superior utility of poetry. This bewilders us today. We cannot conceive a poet being so confident of the intellectual and practical worth of a mere poem.

Such disbelief supports Evelyn Keller's argument summarized above, for it reveals the degree to which we have internalized a masculinized ideal of selfhood founded on separation from nature, rational objectivity, and a need to dominate: individuality as a will to power. Our disbelief also skews contemporary commentary on the ideological functions of romantic poetry. We will misunderstand the politics of the romantic poets so long as we underestimate their conviction of poetry's practical value. This faith in their art's usefulness in teaching interdependency arose from the persuasion that human consciousness is a natural process. Consciousness, they believed, is most effective when most harmoniously attuned to the activities of its nurturing environment. Poetry is the best means for such tempering, the mutually beneficial effects of which will do more for creating good societies than any political dogma.

The romantics would not wish to contradict the current critical banality that "nature" is a social construct (an idea that was already a commonplace to Buffon in the eighteenth century). They would regard the assertion as question-begging, however, because they believed that human consciousness (and the social constructs made possible by it) is a result of natural processes. To criticize and improve social constructs, even of "nature," we must understand how society arises out of humankind's place in the natural world.

The oversimplification of the new historicist claim that "there is no nature" because there is only cultural history obscures the complex dynamics of culture-nature interaction.[27] Raymond Williams began to delineate the historical processes of such interactions years ago in his book *Keywords*, and he developed them in *The Country and the City*. Williams recognized the end of the eighteenth century as a critical moment in the history of the shifting definitions of "nature." From his perspective, new historicists' analyses of Wordsworth's representations of natural phenomena as acts of displacement block any genuine historical understanding of how and why British culture then made what it did of physical environment.

Williams would have us perceive that, because no word is more important in Wordsworth's poetry from 1797 to 1807 than *nature*, the word probably focuses a cultural domain of contestation and transformation. The romantic concern with nature, in fact, manifests a dissolution and reconstitution of conceptual patterns by which natural phenomena had been understood—a process that had begun earlier in the eighteenth century. Wordsworth's poetry is of special value for comprehending this reconstitution because it articulates his unusually keen insight into personal causes of the change in which he was participating.

"Tintern Abbey" (to cite the most obvious example) is structured by the poet's awareness of how different "nature" had been to him at different times in his life, what it now is, and what it might become. Thus:

> nature then
> (The coarser pleasures of my boyish days,
> And their glad animal movements all gone by)
> To me was all in all.
>
> (72–75)

The dramatic affect of the subsequent claim that "Nature never did betray / The heart that loved her" derives from this emphasis on the poet's living in ever-changing relationship to the natural world. His awareness of the differences in his encounters, moreover, implicitly calls into question his culture's generalized conception of nature; "Tintern Abbey" challenges any coercive abstraction of "nature." Not, however, by setting up an oppositional abstract "nature" against the culturally received concept. Wordsworth dramatizes, to the contrary, why our understanding of "nature" must be a mutable one—because what is to be understood are evolving interactions between human beings and environments. This is why I think it helpful to describe the Wordsworthian-romantic position as proto-ecological. For the romantics, cultural history and personal history appear in the form of ever-shifting interrelations with a physically mutable world—interrelations that demand (and reward) self-conscious scrutiny of how we teach ourselves to keep discovering new ways of understanding "nature."

Because the romantic poets believed in the value of enjoyment and the efficacy of poetical pleasures, science for them might sometimes contribute to poetic figurations, but the utility of science must always be limited—may even become dangerous so far as it constricts imaginative

☾ ✲ ✳ ✵

understanding of how human beings best function interdependently among themselves and with their environment. Wordsworth epitomizes this view in his famous "We murder to dissect." Our learning must be holistic, and in the romantic age holism seemed more likely to be achieved by humanism than by science. All the poets, even Keats with his medical training, perceived "scientific" ways of thinking as carrying threats to the poetic imagination needed for the most joyous and most valuable life experiences of both individuals and societies.

I, not they, call the direction of these biases *proto-ecological.* The term is meant to evoke an intellectual position that accepts as entirely real a natural environment existent outside of one's personal psyche. Scientific procedures are useful for helping us to comprehend this reality, because science orders external reality according to systems congenial to a particular society's modes of categorizing. But external reality can be fully appreciated and healthily interacted with only through imaginative acts of mind. The poets, not unjustly in their time, thought of such acts of imagination as beyond the capacity of mere scientists. After all, in their day there was no biochemistry, let alone molecular genetics.

The romantic poets are of special interest to those of us concerned to develop an ecologically oriented criticism exactly because they anticipate—sometimes shrewdly, sometimes absurdly—attitudes and conceptions that only in our century have been given either a solid scientific basis, or whose psychic grounding has only recently been persuasively analyzed. Because the romantics in these respects are in the position of forerunners, they at times seem to us inconsistent, errant and mistaken, very often too speculative. I suspect few biologists are yet ready to follow Wordsworth in believing that plants enjoy emitting oxygen. Yet uninhibited by the enormous mountains of fact piled up by later chemists and biologists, these ecologically oriented poets sometimes direct our attention to essential principles and save us from losing our way among masses of bewildering detail, thereby clarifying why we need an ecological criticism.

As the last poets with strong belief in the practical intellectual, social, and ethical efficacy of acts of imagination, moreover, the romantics display a useful congeniality with thinking of some contemporary scientists and contemporary feminists. These are the intellectuals who have radically reconceived how best to "think scientifically." Their work has increasingly directed attention to problems whose solutions lie in realms distant from those dominated by earlier, more reductively rationalistic adherents of "scientific methods" whose validity has disintegrated under the pressure of accumulated factual knowledge. In many instances, however, recent literary criticism founds itself (usually unconsciously) on such obsolete scientific conceptions and principles.

Contrarily, the picture of how the human brain develops and operates painted in the past decade by Nobel prize winner Gerald M. Edelman is dependent upon an understanding of consciousness as a function of highly individualized brains conceivable only as existing in conditions of continuous interactivity with perpetually changing environments. Such a view, it seems to me, is congruent with Percy Shelley's development of the younger Wordsworth's thinking about the relation of human nature to physical nature. Shelley articulated a more complicated and sociohistorically informed vision of how the human mind and the external natural world were attuned to one another than Wordsworth's. That is why my discussion begins with emphasis on Wordsworth and advances to concentration upon Shelley. This perspective makes possible a highlighting of how romantic poetry articulates a definition of humankind's place in nature not incongruent with that of leading contemporary biologists. To appreciate this "prophetic" success fully, however, we need to have at least a rudimentary awareness of the ways in which today's best biologists conceive of the origin and self-sustaining features of consciousness. My final chapter, therefore, sketches a lay person's understanding of some of the latest neurobiological research into the physical bases of human self-consciousness.

I am willing to give my last pages to an amateurish report of sophisticated scientific research and hypothesizing to illustrate why literary criticism needs to reestablish connections with a wide range of social activities, especially the thinking of contemporary scientists. The increasing self-isolation of criticism within narrow ideological/metaphysical concerns appears to be a defensive maneuver to protect critics from taking up practical social responsibilities. This defensiveness seems to me to arise from their unexamined presupposition expressed in Auden's pessimistic observation that "poetry makes nothing happen," without doing justice to his wonder at what words can accomplish. The "scientific" foundation of most contemporary criticism is a preconception indistinguishable from that favored by the most brutally oversimplifying scientists of the

later nineteenth century who argued for oppressively masculinist conceptions of nature—conceptions which implied that art is practically trivial and of no significance to physical, social, or ethical problems. Poetry, therefore, is a proper subject only of esoteric, academic disputations.

Ecological literary criticism opposes this view (whether explicitly or implicitly expressed) and is sympathetic to the romantic premise that the imaginativeness essential to poetry is the primary human capability enabling us to interact in a responsible manner with our environment. Acts of imagination such as are realized in poems, therefore, may contribute to the resolution of practical social and ethical difficulties, and commentators should endeavor to speak not to an elite or a coterie but to as wide an audience as possible. The romantics never forgot what today we too frequently overlook, that the most important elements of our environment are our fellow human beings—most of whom, thank goodness, are not academic critics.

two

Feminism and the Historicity of Science

In calling for an ecologically oriented criticism I appeal to intensified awareness of the historicity of all our intellectual disciplines. It would seem banal so to appeal, but that Cold War critics, even new historicists, have paid minimal attention to the evolution of our understanding of the natural world, despite their fondness for the truism that conceptions of nature are cultural constructs. An ecological criticism must be historically more self-conscious, if only because ecology is a relative newcomer in the world of science. Such self-consciousness, moreover, is a requisite for any kind of useful interaction between scientific and humanistic studies. It is the dangers of metaphysical universalizing (some of whose disguised self-mystifyings recent feminist critiques have exposed) from which ecologically oriented criticism principally offers to liberate literary studies.

To understand better how this might come about, we need to understand how ecology came into being. The word *ecology* was coined by the zoologist Ernst Haeckel in 1866. Haeckel needed a name for a new science, one just then coming into its own as a systematic discipline. Ecology, he said, was

the body of knowledge concerning the economy of nature—the investigation of the total relations of the animal both to its inorganic and to its

organic environment; including above all, its friendly and inimical relations with those animals and plants with which it comes directly or indi-
rectly into contact—in a word, ecology is the study of all those complex
interrelations referred to by Darwin as the conditions of the struggle for
existence.[1]

Although today there are many diverse forms of scientific ecology whose
practices require refinements or expansions of Haeckel's definition, its
two key features remain undisturbed: ecology treats of total interrelationships of organisms and their environments, and ecology depends
upon Darwinian evolutionary thinking.[2]

These features explain why ecology as a scientific discipline could not
fully emerge before the middle of the nineteenth century. It required the
development of other scientific disciplines. The word *biology*, after all,
entered our language only in the first years of the nineteenth century, just
when chemistry in the form we recognize was attaining its first successes.
Until these studies had achieved systematized efficacy—until, one might
say, there was matured genetics, physiology, and biochemistry—it
remained impossible effectively to develop encompassing studies of the
total interrelations of individual organisms and their environments.

Haeckel asserts ecology's dependence upon Darwin's articulation of
the theory of evolution, which of course emphasizes the temporal
dimension in biological processes. The struggle for existence is a historical struggle, survival of the fittest being survival over time. This
view of nature as temporalized, as existing historically, produces the
seeming paradox of the evolutionary stress upon individuality. Individuality of course had loomed large in Lamarck's evolutionary ideas about
the inheritance of acquired characteristics. The subtler paradox in the
Darwinian focus on variations within populations is illuminated by an
old joke among biologists that *The Origin of Species* destroyed the idea
of species. The joke refers to Darwin's insistence that evolutionary survival depends on any species' being composed of a number of varied
individuals, so that the species can adapt to whatever changes in environment may happen to occur over time. Scientific ecology follows
Darwin by building on the axioms of natural history that every organism is unique but that all organisms and environments are essentially
interdependent.

This understanding of phenomenal reality as constituted of a shifting interdependence of unique historical entities has infected an ever-widening range of disciplines, although humanists have remained until now relatively immune. It is not accidental that the best-known image used to illustrate recent "chaos" theory (which I have already cited) is that of a weather prediction distorted when at a particular moment a single butterfly flaps its wings. Ecological literary criticism would adapt to humanistic studies conceptions of wholeness that—in fashions appropriate to imaginative activities—reaffirm the significance of individuals and individual actions.

So to adapt is not difficult because humanistic interests and humanistic research contributed to the development of ecological ideas. The steady growth from the Renaissance onward of historical studies, especially the development in the eighteenth century of environmental historicism, fostered ecological attitudes. Even the emergence of modern linguistics may have played a part when William Jones at the end of the eighteenth century defined the historical relationship of Sanskrit to Greek and Latin, thereby demonstrating what could be called an evolutionary significance for "extinct species" of languages.[3]

It should not be surprising, therefore, that in British romantic poetry we find significant anticipations of ecological ideas.[4] The anticipations are significant in part because they helped to train imaginations toward receptiveness to ecological conceptions, including the significance of contingency in what Darwin later called the "economy" or, even more strikingly, the "polity" of nature. Because these anticipations did not then (could not then) coalesce into a systematic discipline of thought, they also offer a valuable vantage point from which to question our present, more articulated thinking about the relation of human polities to the polity of nature—including current assumptions about the functions of literature and the responsibilities of its professional critics toward the health of the societies to which they belong.

The special value to literary scholars of such a perspective on their own position is illustrated by the fact that, however extensively ecological ideas have penetrated a variety of sciences, at least one of the principles central to it has been resisted by most contemporary literary critics. They refuse to concentrate attention on the uniqueness of works of art, now symptomatically referring to poems, plays, and novels not as "works" (which is

regarded as foregrounding their individuality) but as "texts." This tendency, which reflects a valuable awareness of the difficulty in rigorously distinguishing text from context, nevertheless requires reexamination, because works of art may fairly be described as the most unique phenomena in all human experience.

Ecological literary criticism, in fact, begins from the presupposition that an essential characteristic of all significant literary works is their uniqueness, not as autonomous artifacts, as the New Criticism regarded them, but as dynamic participants in a constantly self-transforming historical environment—a major component of which is the diverse interpretations to which outstanding works are subjected. Without this premise, it would be impossible to identify in the literary realm the interplay of individuality and interdependence that is the central object of all ecologically oriented studies. The oddest paradox of my insistence on proto-ecological features of British romantic poetry, therefore, is its revelation of how contemporary literary criticism is enfeebled by reliance (largely unconscious) upon postromantic but now obsolete scientific ideas. Such antiquated presuppositions include those that depend on simplistic distinctions between subject (mind) and object (nature), or ignore principles of probability and uncertainty, or fail to recognize the importance of either uniqueness or chance in all life processes. What might be called the premodern "scientificness" of poetry of two hundred years ago, therefore, can help us to understand that humanistic endeavors today have no more powerful (even if often unwitting) supporters than our most innovative scientists, who have overturned cruder, anti-imaginative scientific ideas constituting the concealed intellectual foundation for the principles espoused by many contemporary literary critics.

Let it be absolutely clear, however, that ecological literary criticism does not try to transfer methods of biology, biochemistry, mathematics, or other disciplines to the analysis of literature. It only directs criticism toward examination of the adaptability to humanistic goals of fundamental conceptions that make contemporary ecological studies so important. That examining, however, requires us to reassess the fundamental presuppositions undergirding recent literary theorizing. Such reassessing will, in turn, inevitably compel us into some self-questioning as to the ultimate justifications for our work—for example, what may be the special preciousness (or perniciousness) of specific works of literature and of particular systems of critical commentary that describe and evaluate them.

There is now an enormous literature on scientific ecology, the best orientation into which is provided by Robert P. McIntosh's *The Background of Ecology: Concept and Theory*.[5] McIntosh's work is particularly valuable for its lucid demonstration of why pre–nineteenth century forerunners of ecological thinking remain forerunners of the decisive breakthrough that came during Charles Darwin's lifetime. McIntosh's clarity on this matter is needed. Recent popularizings of "ecology" have encouraged the misapprehension that ecological views have been propounded in Western culture well before the nineteenth century, even by ancient Greeks. Donald Worster, for example, finds the roots of "ecology" in several eighteenth-century writers, including the founder of Methodism, John Wesley. Such "roots" can be found in many places if, like Worster, one uses the term *ecology* in a vague, generalized, and normative sense.[6] Although Clarence Glacken's impressive and comprehensive *The Rhodian Shore* has been used for the same kind of imprecise and inflated ecological rhetoric, Glacken himself explains that he stopped his study at the end of the eighteenth century because "with the 18th century there ends in Western civilization an epoch in the history of man's relationship to nature. What follows is of an entirely different order, influenced by the theory of evolution, specialization in the attainment of knowledge, acceleration in the transformation of nature" (704–5).[7] Current overly generous, if often well intentioned, expansions of "ecology" beyond all specificity of meaning reduce its significance and block our recognition of the potential importance to criticism of developments of the scientific disciplines involved in ecological studies. These developments in the past century have been spectacular. McIntosh's long book, in fact, is little more than a series of condensed descriptions of the varieties of scientific ecology that have begun to flourish in this century. Crucial to all these, it seems fair to say, is "the emphasis upon an holistic approach, which involves the concept of the ecosystem" as "a group of organisms of different kinds . . . with reciprocal relations to the nonliving environment and, especially, having mutual relations of varying kinds and degrees among themselves."[8]

The extraordinary range and vitality of the various kinds of ecological research suggests that, despite the present popularity of "ecological causes," humanists still tend to underestimate the true effects of the emer-

gence of scientific ecology. That conception makes a strong claim to being one of the supreme accomplishments—perhaps finally the greatest—of late nineteenth- and early twentieth-century Western civilization. As an admirer of ancient Greek civilization and for some time now a student of Native American cultures, I have been impressed by these "early" cultures' sensitive understanding of interrelations between human activities and the natural environment—as well as their perceptions into the workings of natural systems. Exemplary is the northern Native American observation that caribou *need* wolves—since wolves are capable of hunting down only ill or weak caribou. But neither ancient Greeks nor Native Americans, nor anyone before the nineteenth century, had, or could have had, a systemically ecological understanding of nature—as the barrenness of the Greek landscape and the abandoned cliff dwellings in the Southwest poignantly testify.

A genuinely ecological understanding is founded on an intricate interplay of sophisticated specialized theorizing with knowledge of detailed scientific facts that could not have been assembled and given unified meaning until well into the last century. Haeckel, for instance, identified four thousand new species of marine protozoa and, like Darwin, made a long voyage on which he became intimately acquainted with the fantastic variety of organisms and meticulously analyzed the often minute but decisive differences between them. Although the spotted owl has served as a means for protecting (at least temporarily) some of this country's virgin Northwest forests from being lumbered off for sale to Japan to make plywood concrete forms, the true environmental importance of the "old" forests is down among their roots, not among their branches. In the decaying of older timber in such forests chemical substances are produced that are necessary to the roots of young trees if they are to absorb nutrients essential to their full maturation. The elimination of older trees makes it impossible for younger ones to grow to maturity. Both the chemical analyses and the knowledge of fundamental biochemical processes required to reconstruct this sequence of causes and effects result from detailed scientific analyses that only a few decades ago became possible through improved technology and the cumulative effect of years of systematized research.

Unless we recognize the complexity of scientific ecology, we fall into cheap sentimentalism that may, in fact, be destructive of our natural environment. Recognizing that ecological thought must be founded on the most advanced, sophisticated, and continuously self-challenging scientific research helps us to assure that scientific work will be productively beneficent. Various sciences have in the past wreaked much destruction on our world, even while doing much good. Especially in our economically globally unified world of the oncoming twenty-first century, the more ecological well-being is made a primary sociocultural aim, the more scientific work can be expected to produce beneficial rather than destructive effects.

Once more a romantic work provides insight into our circumstances by its representation of a situation that foretells with some helpful inaccuracy the problems we confront. Mary Shelley's romantic novel *Frankenstein* (1818) displays the terrible effects of its protagonist creating a "monster" that is a kind of anthropomorphized version of the atomic bomb. The monster may be so described because Victor Frankenstein decides that he will not create a "mate" for the original monster (a hydrogen bomb, so to speak), because the pair might well destroy his species. As I have pointed out elsewhere, this is the first literary presentation of an ethical decision founded on the practical possibility of destruction of the entire human species.[9]

Mary Shelley was able so effectively to foreshadow our fears because in the romantic era for the first time the enormous physical and cultural potency of systematized scientific work had begun to become visible. Her prototypical "mad" scientist begins with a conscious desire to do good. The novel leads us to believe, however, that the terrible consequences of his idealism are rooted in repressed ambiguous impulses and aspirations deriving from unresolved psychosocial problems in his upbringing and education. Victor Frankenstein's "madness" (he is represented as literally "sick") expresses his society's incapacity to direct such idealistic intellectual endeavors as his into paths that will be healthfully useful for both the individual scientist and for his community. The physical "illness" of Shelley's scientist is expressive of the unresolved moral/intellectual contradictions rending him and his society. The kind of contradictions by which Victor Frankenstein is ripped and the kind of ethical struggles in which he is engaged were, in fact, experienced by many physicists associated with the development of nuclear weaponry.

Yet despite this continuing moral relevance of *Frankenstein*, which accounts for the story's sustained popularity and the absorption of its protagonist's name into the common vernacular, Mary Shelley's story strikes many intelligent readers as somewhat silly—a characteristic that helps to explain why the story has been kept alive as much by comedic and parodic versions as by the novel itself or its "serious" dramatizations. Although the conception of Frankenstein's project was not possible before the beginning of the nineteenth century, today his "madness," more significantly than his technology, seems archaic. The simultaneous strength and weakness of Shelley's novel is that in it she displays with perspicuity a central ethical problem endemic to scientific research as it had developed since the Renaissance. But the very progress of science since Shelley's time has to a considerable degree rendered her definition of that problem obsolete.

The underlying ethical dilemma intrinsic to "pure" science deriving from Copernicus and Galileo was that its purity could not exist without absolute freedom. In Shelley's novel the scientist obtains that "freedom" only by surreptitious and basically "subversive" techniques of self-isolation. The significant truth within this melodramatic representation is that scientific practice *is* intellectual experiment and speculation pursued entirely for their own sake. But sophisticated science is also dependent for its full efficacy on the uninhibited flow of information between practitioners, and it is in this regard that Frankenstein's self-isolation, though representative of a psychological truth about scientific research that Wordsworth had already insisted upon,[10] undercuts the relevance of his actions to modern scientific practice.

The development of post-Renaissance science, as I have observed, depended upon its "purity," its freedom from responsibility to the ramifying implications and secondary consequences of its activities. That continued to be the situation into our own century, when the progress of various sciences, especially their increasing need for technological devices requiring economic expenditure beyond the capacity of individuals or local institutions, inevitably carried research across the protective barriers of esoteric thought and private laboratories into continuous, practical, "impure" engagements with social realities. Intellectually, this meant recognition of the limitedness and inherent inadequacy of scientific ideas—signaled by the appearance of Gödel's theorem, Heisenberg's articulation of the uncertainty principle, and, in general, the spreading recognition that physical "laws" applied not to nature in herself but only to nature as experienced and perceived by human beings, awareness that "nature" must be to a considerable degree a construct of particular cultural assumptions. So today, the best physicists are ready to say that much of what they have discovered seems absurd and self-contradictory.[11] Yet physically, the progress of science brought it to the point where it could not function without financial and physical support of society so massive as to compel scientists constantly to justify their activities to ordinary citizens. This has meant defining for themselves and others all the ramifying implications and consequences of their research. Science today can sustain its integrity as science only by violating its original "purity," by finding its freedom not by isolating itself but by pursuing its special concerns through intense exploration of how those concerns shape and are shaped by the total socionatural contexts within which alone its work becomes possible.

That the rise of ecology is coincidental with this transformation of science from "private" to "public" activity is no accident. The developmental progress of each of the sciences inevitably carried each toward what may fairly be termed ecological orientations. What happened in a sense was simply an inversion of the scientists' starting point. The contemporary scientist, unlike Victor Frankenstein, begins his research on the basis of a definition, usually implicit but sometimes quite explicit, of its probable consequences—which normally takes the form of writing a successful grant application. Thus, in theory anyway, a scientist begins by entering into a socially contractual process by which the value of the work proposed, however esoteric, even seemingly absurd, is determined within a larger social context. As important, this system of defining the validity of science through its interactions with the realities of nonscientific natural and cultural worlds is founded on an assumption of incompleteness and uncertainty. The fundamental presupposition of contemporary scientists is that neither their work nor their work in conjunction with that of their colleagues will produce absolutely final answers. The aim now of most practicing scientists is not, as Victor Frankenstein's was, an ultimately definitive revelation, "*the* secret of life." Exactly because such definitive explanations are seen as illusory, scientists now tend increasingly to value their work in terms of a particular, let us call it temporary, relation to an

ever-changing complex of natural processes, which are likely to be modified in unpredictable ways by their own work.

This is why professional scientists are often leading spokespersons insisting that the potential impact and influence of scientific experiments and inventions must be—and can be—carefully assessed *before* work is begun. A fundamental attraction of ecological thinking is that it provides a basis on which the nonspecialist may usefully join in making such assessments. Until our own era, society's fundamental difficulty with scientific "progress" was discovering efficacious means for judging whether a certain kind of process ought from the point of view of social benefit to be pursued or blocked or postponed. The emergence of scientific ecology provides such means acceptable to both specialists and lay persons. Responsible scientists can accept the legitimacy of the question "What is that going to do to my lawn next year?" That is, they can accept the responsibility for answering queries as to their work's effects in terms satisfactory to nonspecialist lawn-owners.

There are, of course, plenty of profound disagreements. But the disagreements testify to the existence now of possibilities for common ground. Ecological issues are, moreover, especially appropriate subjects for democratic debate and decision. The weighing of diverse aspects and complex balances of positive and negative factors for the community as a whole are precisely what a free, responsible citizenry can best do. As scientists will rightly insist, expert knowledge is necessary; but no leading scientists claim any longer that the specialist is the only one who should decide on what is good or bad for the community. And so far as the community fully recognizes its responsibilities, these cannot be solely toward its own welfare as an isolated entity but must also include assessments of the interdependence of its welfare with that of other communities, both cultural and natural.

Negative illustrations from our own century of the congruence of democratic procedures and ecological responsibility are, of course, the spectacular collapse in pollution—ecocide, as it has been called—of Marxist regimes in Eastern Europe, and the official ecological programs of the Nazis. The Nazi experience is especially illuminating because it is so confusing. Unquestionably, ecological ideals, or ecologically tinged ideas, were important for many of the Nazi leaders and administrators—Hitler's vegetarianism and Himmler's support of animal rights (Himmler

31

was responsible for the promulgation of antivivisection laws) have been well publicized. Rudolph Hess was a follower of Rudolph Steiner, the anthroposophist who was an influential propagandist for organic farming; and Walter Darré, Hitler's first minister of agriculture, supported members of his ministry who succeeded in blocking plans for land reclamation and moorland drainage to preserve wild countryside, and vigorously espoused reforestation projects, even in Poland when that country was overrun by the German army. Nor were these results of mere personal idiosyncrasy, for, as Bramwell observes, although opposing left-wing and liberal convictions that nature and its laws could, and should, be transcended by human society, at the same time "the nazis opposed capitalism and the consumer-oriented market mechanism. In theory, if not in practice, they supported critiques of mercantilism, and claimed to serve ideals of long-term responsibility, duty, and service for the community."[12] Yet, although these ecological orientations drew heavily on a variety of pre-Nazi German intellectual and social traditions, before the fall of the Third Reich most of its significant ecological initiatives had been abandoned or grossly perverted.

Such a summary does no justice to the contradictory complexity of ecological-ideological forces in Nazi Germany, a contradictory complexity that has carried over into subsequent German "Green" political movements, but it allows one to suggest that there may be an inherent incompatibility between antidemocratic political systems and increasingly sophisticated ecological conceptions. Ecological holism, as I have already pointed out, with its inherent respect for individualities, seems on the face of it uncongenial with elitist, dictatorial, bureaucratic ideologies. Reciprocally, some of the scientific fields central to ecological thought are beginning to display responsiveness to "democratizing" tendencies.

Evelyn Keller has with extraordinary subtlety and persuasiveness described such a change through analyses of the fate of some of her own genetic research and of Barbara McClintock's career. The latter is distinguished by the recognition of her success only after long years of being marginalized in her discipline. McClintock's research showing that genetic sequences are not fixed was disregarded because it ran counter to the "central dogma" in genetics for two decades following the discovery of the structure of DNA. The dogma was that DNA was the dictatorial executive governor of cellular organization, with information flowing one way,

always from, never to, the DNA. That it had, indeed, become dogma is revealed by Jacques Monod's Frankensteinian assertion in the 1968: "The Secret of Life? But this is in large part known—in principle, if not in details."

Keller observes that "the central dogma was without question inordinately successful as well as scientifically productive"; that the dogma "ultimately proved inadequate," however, demonstrates for her "that its trouble lay deeper than just a too hasty generalization from the simple to the complex; its presumptuousness, I suggest, was built into its form of explanation."[13] That form, Keller, argues, is essentially a creation of male-gendered thinking. Keller's claim is for something much more complex and interesting than that Barbara McClintock practiced "feminist science," or would even tolerate the suggestion that her research was in any sense "a woman's work," or that "her views represent a woman's perspective." In the first place, as Keller pointed out in her biography of McClintock, her eventual vindication "demonstrates the capacity of science to overcome its own characteristic kinds of myopia, reminding us that its limitations do not reinforce themselves indefinitely. Their own methodology allows, even obliges, scientists to continually reencounter phenomena even their best theories cannot accommodate" (197). Nevertheless, Keller argues, the history of McClintock's slow acceptance by her discipline proves that

> because she is not a man, in a world of men, her commitment to a gender-free science has been binding; because concepts of gender have so deeply influenced the basic categories of science, that commitment has been transformative . . . the relevance of McClintock's gender in this story is to be found not in her role in her personal socialization but precisely in the role of gender in the construction of science. (174)

McClintock's story, Keller justly observes, required a redefining of the unspoken assumption underlying science that it consists in "the naming of object (nature) as female and the parallel naming of subject (mind) as male" (174), so that nature is "renamed as not female, or at least, as not an alienated object." Simultaneously, "mind must be renamed as not necessarily male, and, accordingly, recast with a more inclusive subjectivity" (175).

The nature of that subjectivity has been eloquently described by McClintock herself, as when she describes her state of mind that led to her view that "one cannot consider the genes as all important" in themselves (as the "central dogma" held) but that they "are organized functional units, whose very function is defined by their position in the organization as a whole" and that they function "only with respect to the environment in which [they are] found" (168). McClintock then describes the subjective aspect of her work that enabled her to identify chromosomes among which she had previously not been able to distinguish.

> I found that the more I worked with them, the bigger and bigger [the chromosomes] got, and when I was really working with them I wasn't outside. I was down there. I was part of the system. I was right down there with them, and everything got big. I even was able to see the internal parts of the chromosomes—actually everything was there. It surprised me because I actually felt as if I was right down there and these were my friends. . . . As you look at these things, they become part of you. And you forget yourself."[14]

This attitude of humble intimacy, of passing through the artificial constructs of subject-object distinction, should strike a profoundly responsive chord in some literary critics. It is analogous, at any rate, to my own experience in reading poetry. That experience is one of empathetic engagement, of being caught up with the emotional development of the words, a paradoxical loss of self in an enhancement of subjective emotionalized understanding. It is to this learned capability of responsiveness that I attribute my pleasure in rereading fine poetry endlessly, always finding new surprises and wonders, amazed at how much I had before more than looked in what I thought were familiar lines. That my experience is not merely idiosyncratic I deduce from the fact that the colleagues I most admire seem, like me, unable to make much use of old notes when teaching familiar poems.

Ecologically oriented humanists, I therefore believe, could, as well as receiving the benefit of inspiration from scientific studies, perhaps contribute to some productive attitudes in scientists. Feminists like Keller have already done so. Other feminists might have similar impact if they worked from a more informed understanding of the total cultural histo-

ry of the interplay between scientific and humanistic studies. There has been a tendency, manifest in a work such as Carolyn Merchant's *The Death of Nature*,[15] for example, to treat all post-Renaissance science as a metaphysical monolith. This mistake, which fails to recognize (as Keller does) the historical as well as the intrinsically pluralistic nature of science, limits the effectiveness of such critiques. Their value as needed criticisms could be enriched by a better understanding, to choose an instance dear to my heart, of the interactions between scientific and literary innovations during the romantic era. That interactivity eloquently testifies to the importance of science's historicity, a historicity to which an ecological criticism must constantly call attention. Indeed, it seems to me that the broadest intellectual significance of work by scientists such as Barbara McClintock or Gerald M. Edelman will be generally underestimated, or far too slowly made use of, so long as we lack humanistic scholarship that encourages specialists in the arts, language, and culture to concern themselves in a fashion appropriate to their disciplines to both past and concurrent historical self-transformations of scientific research. Ecological criticism cannot be genuinely holistic unless it functions in awareness of—among other things—its reciprocal relationship to the natural sciences. The emergence of feminist thinking, as well as some recent developments in anthropology, should foster that awareness, even as the breakdown of modernist political systems and the formation of new global economic interconnections demand reevaluation of our traditional modes of cultural commentary and analysis.

Ecological criticism, of course, cannot be ideologically neutral any more than it can exist independent of specific metaphysical presuppositions. Every ecologically oriented critic must, like his or her fellows, work from criticizable political and philosophical assumptions that significantly limit his or her perspective. This book will certainly reveal my prejudices, most obviously on the political side, skepticism of much contemporary Marxist thinking and a preference for democratic institutions as they have developed in America. On the metaphysical side, my conviction should be as apparent that there exists a real, phenomenal world of nature (not ruled by any transcendent deity and not solely a cultural construct) of which physicists, chemists, and biologists give us good if necessarily inadequate descriptions, and that some understanding of this natural world's history is now a prerequisite to useful evaluations of significant cultural achievements. Because ecological criticism seeks to foster such understanding, it is only secondarily concerned with issues of ideology, although (as I suggest in my final chapter) it does encourage more cosmopolitan and less parochially defensive attitudes toward current political and ethnic problems. There are, to be sure, grave dangers in the globalized perspective I recommend, yet one may hope that the risks of cosmopolitanism are minimal when it is based on a commitment to the importance of the physical world of nature in all its dynamic concreteness. Without ecological understanding, E. M. Forster's dark vision of a single globalizing culture may be all too prophetic: "Under cosmopolitanism, if it comes, we shall receive no help from the earth. Trees and meadows and mountains will only be a spectacle, and the binding force that they once exercised on character must be entrusted to Love alone."[16]

three

Surprised by Nature: Ecology and Cold War Criticism

Jonathan Bate dedicates his book *Romantic Ecology* to the proposition that "the way in which William Wordsworth sought to enable his readers better to enjoy or to endure life was by teaching them to look at and dwell in the natural world."[1] He describes the historical circumstances now producing a need to revive this ecological message from England's most important romantic poet. As I indicated in my first chapter, Bate portrays "new historicist" romantic criticism as reactive—especially against formalist "Yale School" critics, Geoffrey Hartman, Paul de Man, and Harold Bloom, who in the 1960s had influentially attacked the traditional understanding of the romantics as "poets of nature."

Paul de Man found the essential accomplishment of Wordsworth's *Prelude* to be the establishing of the poet's consciousness as independent "of all relationship with the outside world." Hartman more subtly argued for the autonomy of Wordsworth's imagination, "its independence . . . from strong outward stimuli," its "transcendence of Nature."[2] In portentous language Harold Bloom offered equivalent claims for the potency of a transcendent imagination in Blake and Shelley. The core of the new historicist reaction against these views (which Bate rightly sees triggered by Jerome J. McGann) accepts the Yale assumption that the romantic poets sought transcendence. New historicists, however, explain that quest as a guilt-ridden expression of a concealed "reactionary" political ideology. Servilely following Louis Althusser's claim of "literature's servility to ideology," McGann in *Romantic Ideology* set new historicists on a track of rarefied Marxian analyses.[3] These critics find references to natural phenomena in romantic poetry to be psychological "displacements" of ideological anxieties. So in Wordsworth's "Ode: Intimations of Immortality" the single tree and field, Marjorie Levinson insists, refer to the French Liberty Tree and the Champ de Mars, whereas Alan Liu roundly asserts that for romantic poetry "there is no nature."[4]

Bate's history of romantic criticism recognizes an underlying flow of critical continuity beneath oppositions that calls for a radically new angle of vision provided by ecological criticism. A link between the Yale School and Marxist new historicists lies in their common presuppositions, first, that romantic poets regarded private consciousness as distinct from and superior to all natural phenomena, and second, that the poets regularly sought to transcend, if only linguistically, the physical circumstances of their experiences in the natural world. Both sets of critics undervalue romantic counterconceptions of the individual self as fully existent only in relation to other selves, and of human nature as significantly determined by natural environment. Both sets of critics avert their eyes from the poets' insistence that imaginative consciousness is best understood in terms of its adaptations to—and therefore its power to *transform* rather than transcend—the actualities of humankind's physical environment—of which continuing relations with other human beings are a primary feature. Had Wordsworth, for example, ended "Tintern Abbey" at line 111, before introducing his sister (as recent critics would seem to prefer), the poem could not develop its underlying contrast of the poet's present situation with his first view by himself of the scene in late July five years earlier.[5] Upon this contrast between loneliness and relationship is built his assessment of humankind's fittedness in the natural scheme of things.

An ecologically oriented criticism directs itself to understanding persistent romantic struggles to articulate meaningful human relations within the conditions of a natural world in which transcendence is not at issue. Such criticism does not dismiss the copious evidence of romantic claims that imaginative consciousness fulfills, rather than contravenes, the dynamic tendencies of natural life. Ecologically oriented criticism

thus recognizes a foreshadowing of its own understanding of humanity's relation to nature in the romantic view that it is natural for human beings to be self-conscious, and natural, therefore, to construct their cultures out of complexly interassimilative engagements with their physical and biological environment. Foreshadowings of this kind are valuable, because they enable literary scholars to define with precision how their critical presuppositions have differentially emerged from the cultural discourse of their predecessors.

As I pointed out in the first chapter, Marxist new historicists have argued that Yale critics disregarded ideological commitments of paramount importance to romantic poets. The poets suffered, McGann claims in *The Romantic Ideology*, from the illusion that "poetry, or even consciousness, can set one free of the ruins of history and culture" (91). McGann the unillusioned contemporary Marxist, however, recognizes that such self-deceptions betray the poets' unavailing efforts to escape their repressed guilt for having abandoned their original political idealism, which favored the aims of the French Revolution. The Yale critics, concentrating on formalistic issues, missed this ideological guiltiness because it had been repressed. When, for example, Wordsworth's poetry overtly refers to a natural object, his covert purpose is to articulate symbolically an anxiously hidden, subconscious political-economic motive.

This view of the concealed "politicizing" of romantic poetry, of course, derives from Marxist conceptions of ideology, originating in Marx's view of the overriding importance to the character of human societies of their modes of economic production. That was a view of which, as Jonathan Bate has observed in *Romantic Ecology*, romantic poets were keenly skeptical (9, 57). The observation implies a deeper coherence between romantic poetics and romantic politics that the new historicists' stress upon personal psychology for its own purposes has displaced.

We need, therefore, to consider the latent rather than manifest significance of recent critics' determination to deny the romantics' profound concern with the natural world. Unconsciously expressing attitudes of superpower oppositionalism deriving from the global situation produced by the second World War, as I suggested in the first chapter, these critics extend Cold War psychology into literary scholarship. Their secret bias is manifested in the polemical character of their writings, violent to the point of apocalypticness, symptomatic of the political "we-them" mentality dominant in the United States and the Soviet Union for nearly half a century. To these critics, "power" is all-important. They identify criticism as an act of violence, in a vocabulary drawn from war: "strategy," "tactics," and the like are deployed against hostile opponents, with insinuated condemnations of unnamed "traditional humanists" reminding one of Senator McCarthy's "exposure" of fantasized communists. The Cold War mentality defines "others" as enemies, because it perceives all relations, even those of academic scholarship, in terms of struggles for power. These critics carry into the realm of literary commentary and theorizing the ethos of Nietzsche: "Life itself is *essentially* appropriation, injury, overpowering of what is alien and weaker; suppression, hardness, imposition of one's own forms, incorporation and at the least, at its mildest, exploitation."[6]

Paradoxically, these power-obsessed critics, as Bate has remarked, seem to welcome their political irrelevance, often going out of their way to affirm their practical social impotence. Their distaste for ordinary language and their preference for esoteric jargons may be read as symptomatic of a subconscious desire to escape from the responsibilities of involvement with real and "hot" socioeconomic problems. The use of abstract formulations to obscure concrete problems is not an unfamiliar phenomenon, but it is especially characteristic of these pseudocombatants. By not heating up, by not becoming real combat, the Cold War encouraged unrisky indulgence in theoretical violence and a language of hostility, especially among those comfortably cushioned against the impingement of actual suffering. Harold Bloom's strangely aggressive vocabulary appears designed to assure academia's detachment from the savagery of urban streets. McGann's manipulations of Frankfurt Marxism seems only a subtler device for forestalling engagement with practical economic problems. Like the engineers and planners developing top-secret star-war systems of mass destruction, high-tech literary theorists enter into debates with themselves far too abstract to be connected with specific and immediate realities of injustice, poverty, and devastation of the natural environment.

It is to such immediate specificities that Jonathan Bate attributes the development of his criticism, citing the importance of his hikes through landscape familiar to Wordsworth and Ruskin now ominously dominat-

ed by nuclear processing plants. The end of the Cold War and the explosive reemergence of diverse nationalisms within a globalized but increasingly unbalanced economy offers an opportunity to break free of our criticism's commitment to binary oppositionalism and esoteric isolationism. We are now admirably (if dangerously) positioned to explore ways of making literary criticism more practically relevant to lives and environments of ordinary people. This is a moment in which we may discover feelings analogous to the romantics' enthusiastic wonder at the multiple alternatives confronting societies in upheaval. We may now anticipate the excitement of trying to choose among different possibilities for making the earth a better place than a desolately crowded scene of alienated narcissists. To seize this opportunity, however, demands a willingness to recapture something of the romantic high value for ambivalent feelings and localized individuality of experience in preference to the promulgation of "universal" laws. The intellectual universalizing so characteristic of academic criticism in recent years is tightly bound into will-to-power oppositional thinking—thinking that offers the dark, secret pleasure of projecting aggressive emotions in the guise of an impersonalized rationality. It is all too satisfying thus through a vocabulary of abstract reasoning to fabricate opponents, "others" assumed to be filled with enmity, over whom one's ideas will "triumph"—in precisely the negative sense that Shelley uses the word in his last poem.

McGann's claim in *The Romantic Ideology*, for instance, that the romantic poets regarded themselves as imprisoned within "ruins of history and culture" (91) reveals how scholarly casualness may cloak unconscious purposes in distorting the romantic situation by imposing on it a contemporary mind-set. However accurate McGann's phrase might be of T. S. Eliot at the end of the first World War, the evidence is overwhelming that his phrase is grotesquely inappropriate to the circumstances of the English romantic poets. As scholars as different as Alan Bewell, Marilyn Butler, and Larry J. Swingle have demonstrated, English romantic poets confronted a daunting array of alternatives released by the explosive force of new ideas, new political aspirations, new technological developments.[7] It was the multiple opportunities of an expansive flowering of "history and culture" that dazzled (and at times confused) the romantics. "Bliss was it in that dawn to be alive," Wordsworth famously exulted,

41

"But to be young was very heaven." Romantics lamenting imprisonment among ruins is a middle-aged fantasy of Marxism fetishized, a fantasy forgetful of even how many romantics enjoyed ruins.

Social and economic historians have long recognized the romantic era as the apex of a great watershed: the transformation of the agricultural basis of European civilization to an industrial foundation—with England in the vanguard of the change. [8] This was the first time in history when the possibility that mankind might free itself from utter dependence upon the natural world became realistically conceivable. One must emphasize, however, the tentative aspects of this situation at the end of the eighteenth century. Industrialization was then only in its initial stages, and no sane person at that time thought natural forces could be disregarded.

Indeed, no one old enough to remember life before antibiotics will march under the new historicist banner "There is no nature." Nor should anyone who has encountered a forest fire, sailed on the ocean, or been out in a middle-western thunderstorm. Certainly people of the romantic era felt profound respect for and awe of the natural world. Because of that awe and respect their perception of possibilities for channeling, harnessing, directing parts of nature for the benefit of humankind was bewilderingly exciting. The outstanding difference, for example, between graphic representations of sublimity in the mid–eighteenth century and those of the romantic era is the latter's frequent representations of natural phenomena associated with industrialization. Much of the special power of the work of J.M.W. Turner and John Constable, for example, lies in their mingling (of course in quite different ways) of natural and industrial-technological circumstances.

The romantics took for granted neither natural powers nor the technological powers of industrialized culture.

The multiple possibilities of their social circumstances, which demanded rethinking humankind's fundamental relationship to the natural world, partly accounts for the romantics' proto-ecological attitudes. Building upon Enlightenment environmental historicism and the beginnings of modern anthropological conceptions, the romantics perceived particular cultures as defined by the peculiar manner in which each society adapts itself to specific physical circumstances. They created the idea of a "natural" patriotism—loyalty to country referring to

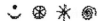

both political state and geographical locale. The romantics' thinking, however, was made intricate by their inheriting from the Enlightenment a very complex (rather than a simple) conception of what "nature" and natural circumstances were—which they then further complicated and enriched.

The inherited complexity was rooted in a dual and basically contradictory vision. On the one hand there was what may be called the macroscopic vision of nature as an indifferent mechanism of cosmic physical forces. On the other hand, there was the microscopic view of the natural world as the wonderfully contingent play of minutely particularized biochemical processes. This double vision, a simultaneous superimposition of contradictory perspectives, is the perspective within which "the meanest flower that blows" may for Wordsworth evoke "thoughts too deep for tears."

This dual vision of nature compelled the romantics to examine with intensified self-consciousness how they responded both to what nature makes of us and to what we make of it—and what we *might* make of it and it of us. The results of such examining could never be simply conclusive, definitive. For one thing, the romantics regarded the natural cosmos, even in its astronomical, mechanistic aspect, as inherently vital. What is alive is continually self-transforming. For another thing, they emphasized the pleasurableness of being alive. They regarded natural processes as being *intrinsically* joyous—which of course only increases the pain of one's consciousness of the inevitability of death.

The romantic poets persistently assert that poetic composition arises out of pleasure, and as unfailingly they insist on the pleasure of reading or hearing poetry. This emphasis, of course, contrasts to our contemporary assumption that poetry originates in injury, illness, unhappiness, and significantly yet duplicitously expresses mostly fears and anxieties. Recent critics tend to distort the romantic "pleasure aesthetic" by imposing on the earlier poets a fashionably complacent pseudopessimism. This mistake is easy to make if one ignores how the romantics differ from us in defining the relations between natural and cultural processes. They could think of natural processes, in the first place, as inherently delightful because life-sustaining in their transformativeness. The most explicit statement of this attitude is found in Wordsworth's lyric "Lines Written in Early Spring."

I heard a thousand blended notes,
While in a grove I sate reclined,
In that Sweet mood when pleasant thoughts
Bring sad thoughts to the mind.

To her fair works did nature link
The human soul that through me ran;
And much it griev'd my heart to think
What man has made of man.

Through primrose-tufts, in that sweet bower,
The periwinkle trail'd its wreathes;
And 'tis my faith that every flower
Enjoys the air it breathes.

The birds around me hopp'd and play'd,
Their thoughts I cannot measure,
But the least motion which they made,
It seem'd a thrill of pleasure.

The budding twigs spread out their fan,
To catch the breezy air;
And I must think, do all I can,
That there was pleasure there.

If I these thoughts may not prevent,
If such be of my creed the plan,
Have I not reason to lament
What man has made of man?[9]

The first point to notice about this poem is that Wordsworth's "faith" is not presented as evidence of any transcendent divinity or divine force. His faith is "naturalistic." He describes what in "Michael" he calls the "pleasure which there is in life itself." The foundation for his proto-ecological conception of the natural cosmos, therefore, is grounded in thoroughly materialistic perceptions.

Characteristic of this view is Wordsworth's tentativeness, his willing-

ness to write a poem that hypothesizes. Here—as in so many of his lyrics—*if* is a key word. It is his "faith"—not his sure knowledge—that every flower "enjoys the air it breathes." The birds' motions "seemed"—not were—"a thrill of pleasure." He "must think, do all I can" that the twigs feel pleasure in the breeze. The poet finds himself *constrained* to entertain the notion of the twigs' pleasure. The phrase "do all I can" suggests that his present intuition contradicts everything that he has been taught about how plants and humans relate—that, for instance, "we" are sentient as "they" are not. His experience of natural phenomena, however, forces him to resist his education, his cultural training, just as his poem challenges our learned cultural presupposition that human consciousness alienates us from physical nature.

His experience can so affect him because the poet believes that nature links "the human soul that through me ran" to her own "fair works." I take it that by the odd phrasing—the "human soul" running "through" him—the poet implies a quality or character of natural humanness that underlies all diverse cultures. All human cultures are constructed by natural creatures. This reading gives added resonance to the famous line "what man has made of man." Why the poet be should grieved by "what man has made of man" may be plain enough for anyone who knows anything about human history. In the context of this experience of the natural world, however, it seems fair to say that the line suggests not only how we fight with, degrade, and destroy one another but also how such self-injuries may be rooted in a miseducation of ourselves away from linkages through pleasure with beneficent natural processes.

The final stanza ends, in characteristic romantic fashion, with a question, not because the poet is pessimistic but because in a complex world of multiple possibilities absolute certainty is rare, and a demand for it can be dangerously constricting. As so often in romantic poetry, the poet also puts a burden of active decision making on the reader. As the poet questions himself and sees more than one possibility of meaning in his experience of his environment, so he wants his reader to question and test the experience of the poem—to consider the different possibilities it raises. In this lyric, for example, what does uncapitalized "heaven" in the final stanza mean? What may be its relation to "Nature's holy plan?" These intimations complicate the poet's querying the "reason to lament," when the crux of his experience is an intuition that natural being is pleasure, that the flowers around him are enjoying the process of their transpiration.

One quite reasonable response to the poet's query is to judge his faith misplaced. The flowers and the birds and the twigs do not feel any pleasure; the poet has only attributed that enjoyment to them. Is it not rather silly to think of little periwinkles happily taking in carbon dioxide and sending out oxygen? I believe that the tendency of many readers so to respond is checked by the line "what man has made of man." We may not know exactly what the phrase means, but probably most of us would hesitate to declare it silly to deplore what human beings have done to themselves. Many of us, at any rate, feel that too much of human history is lamentable—gratuitously lamentable. If a reader's mind goes this far, he or she almost inevitably begins to reconsider the lyric, to wonder if perhaps part of our troubles arise because our cultures cut us off from a joyous vitality offered to us by natural phenomena as natural creatures as well as cultural beings.

If we consider that possibility we have, I believe, been affected as Wordsworth hoped we would be. He does not know, he is not certain. He only reports what he has hypothesized and imagined from a concrete physical experience, from what he has discovered about nature and human conceptions of nature of its possible value. But any readers in the 1990s aware of environmental problems caused by the destruction of oxygen-producing plants are unlikely to dismiss the lyric as nonsensical. Whatever Wordsworth may have meant by his phrase "what man has made of man," some of us will recognize that it is not an inappropriate evocation of how cultures can be self-injuring, not least through wasting, polluting, and destroying an environment that has fostered the development of our species. This response is not merely a modern imposition. Not only the natural scene described in the lyric but also the deliberate vagueness of Wordsworth's memorable phrase helps to evoke thought and feeling about "political" actions neither excluded from nor confined to immediate, particular, transient ideological conflicts.

In the foregoing comments I have tried to illustrate the tentativeness of ecological literary criticism. Committed simultaneously to the importance of the poem as a unique entity and to its existence within a holistically conceived environment, an ecological critic must try in interpreting to take into account the fashion in which a fine poem always exceeds any

interpretation, is a fine poem because not containable within a single reading. Ecological criticism, instead of defining itself against some other metaphysical position, endeavors to sustain the poem's resistance to the imposition of any definitive interpretation and thereby through criticism to renew its vital, hence changing, meaningfulness. Ecological criticism sustains the possibility of cultural discovery as well as of invention.

The need for a criticism consciously resistant to what Wordsworth called "that most dreadful enemy to our pleasures, our own pre-established codes of decision," those "codes of fraud and woe" as Shelley termed them, stands forth boldly when we confront romantic poetry.[10] Wordworth's faith in life's intrinsic pleasurableness was held in conjunction with his antithetical awareness of nature as a dauntingly vast, ever-ongoing system implacably indifferent to the fate of particular parts of it. The conjunction, in fact, is the essentially ambivalent romantic vision of nature. The paradigmatic expression of this antithesis, if resolvable, only through ecological conceptions, is of course Wordsworth's "A Slumber Did My Spirit Seal." A sure instinct has led almost every commentator to treat this as a central Wordsworthian poem. In fact, this lyric's dark vision of the blindness brought upon ourselves by our delighted absorption in another human being, by our wonderfully dangerous capacity for intense personal affection for another or for others, is at the root of *all* romantic poetry.

> A slumber did my spirit seal,
> I had no human fears:
> She seem'd a thing that could not feel
> The touch of earthly years.
>
> No motion has she now, no force
> She neither hears nor sees
> Roll'd round in earth's diurnal course
> With rocks and stones and trees![11]

The painful personal experience presented within a cosmic setting of sublime indifference epitomized in "A Slumber" echoes everywhere throughout romantic poetry, first and most famously perhaps in Wordsworth's own "Tintern Abbey." There the poet asserts his faith that "nature never did betray the heart that loved her," even while explicitly recognizing that nature will kill him (146–49). An equivalent emotional antithesis reappears in Byron's last complete narrative poem, *The Island*, written more than two decades later. In this poem the lushly sensual personal fulfillment of Torquil and the native girl Neuha in their sea grotto is dramatically juxtaposed with the death of Fletcher Christian and his fellow mutineers on the edge of the enduringly indifferent ocean.

> Cold lay they where they fell, and weltering,
> While o'er them flapp'd the sea-birds' dewy wing,
> Now wheeling nearer from the neighboring surge,
> And screaming high their harsh and hungry dirge:
> But calm and careless heaved the wave below,
> Eternal with unsympathetic flow;
> Far o'er its face the dolphins sported on,
> And sprung the flying fish against the sun,
> Till its dried wing relapsed from its brief height,
> To gather moisture for another flight.[12]
>
> (4.13.363–72)

This sublimely inhuman perspective upon the sensationally romantic fulfillment of Torquil and Neuha's natural impulses exemplifies how essential to the "romantic vision of nature" is its antitranscendental bias. Perhaps the most vivid illustration is provided by another very familiar passage from Wordsworth's poetry, the conclusion of "The Ruined Cottage." No single poem has more encouraged the modern predilection for early versions of Wordsworth poems (now enshrined in the Cornell Wordsworth series for worship by textual primitivists). No contrast could be starker than the Pedlar's advice to the poet in the original version as against his revised admonition as the Wanderer in the published version that appeared in the first book of *The Excursion*. In the revision the Wanderer not only offers the poet Christian consolation but also claims that Margaret, the wretched protagonist of his story, was sustained by her faith in Christ.

> The Old Man, noting this, resumed, and said,
> "My Friend! enough of sorrow you have given,
> The purposes of wisdom ask no more:
> Nor more would she have craved as due to One

Who, in her worst distress, had ofttimes felt
The unbounded might of prayer; and learned, with soul
Fixed on the Cross, that consolation springs,
From sources deeper far than deepest pain,
For the meek sufferer. Why then should we read
The forms of things with an unworthy eye?
She sleeps in the calm earth, and peace is here.
I well remember that those very plumes,
Those weeds, and the high spear-grass on that wall,
By mist and silent rain-drops silvered o'er,
As once I passed, into my heart conveyed
So still an image of tranquillity,
So calm and still, and looked so beautiful
Amid the uneasy thoughts which filled my mind,
That what we feel of sorrow and despair
From ruin and from change, and all the grief
that passing shows of Being leave behind,
Appeared an idle dream, that could maintain,
Nowhere, dominion o'er the enlightened spirit
Whose meditative sympathies repose
Upon the breast of Faith."

(931–55)

In the earlier version the Pedlar offers only the mysterious tranquility of
mind that came upon him when seeing raindrops on the same weeds and
speargrass growing through Margaret's decayed house that his companion
has contemplated, advising the poet:

Be wise and cheerful, and no longer read
The forms of things with an unworthy eye.
She sleeps in the calm earth, and peace is here.
I well remember that those very plumes,
Those weeds, and the high spear-grass on that wall,
By mist and silent raindrops silver'd o'er,
As once I passed did to my heart convey
So still an image of tranquillity,
So calm and still, and looked so beautiful

> Amid the uneasy thoughts which filled my mind,
> That what we feel of sorrow and despair
> From ruin and from change, and all the grief
> The passing shews of being leave behind,
> Appeared an idle dream that could not live
> Where meditation was. I turned away
> And walked along my road in happiness.
>
> (510–25)[13]

Like every other modern reader I know of, I find the original infinitely more powerful and moving than the revision. Yet *how* does the early version so effectively portray a believable serenity of mind? How can observation of the simplest natural phenomena, raindrops on weeds, satisfy us after our feelings have been harrowed by representations of the indifferent destructiveness of natural processes? The Christian consolation eliminates that paradox, to the detriment of poetic effect, because the thrust of Wordsworth's story is to compel us to recognize the ambivalence intrinsic to the special self-awareness of "human nature." His original conclusion, for example, tragically realizes the insight expressed earlier by the Pedlar when he breaks off his story.

> He said, "'Tis now the hour of deepest noon.
> At this still season of repose and peace,
> This hour when all things which are not at rest
> Are cheerful; while the multitude of flies
> With tuneful hum is filling all the air;
> Why should a tear be on an Old Man's cheek?
> Why should we thus, with an untoward mind,
> And in the weakness of humanity,
> From natural wisdom turn our hearts away;
> To natural comfort shut our eyes and ears;
> And, feeding on disquiet, thus disturb
> The calm of nature with our restless thoughts?"
>
> (36)

The Pedlar's point is that nature never withdraws its fundamental beneficence; this is the sense in which nature does not betray. Humankind—

for reasons made anguishingly comprehensible by Margaret's suffering—
is constantly drawn into resisting what connects us to the beneficence of
natural vitality. Wordsworth, as the revision illustrates, could not himself
sustain his original naturalistic, materialistic ambivalence. He retreated to
unambiguous Christian consolation, justifying Shelley's accusation in
"Peter Bell the Third" that he was too weak to bear the full potency of the
truths of nature, complex, paradoxical truths that he had once been
strong enough to evoke powerfully.

The bitterness of Shelley's recrimination, however, springs from the
younger poet's profound, and by no means unconscious, indebtedness to
Wordsworth.[14] Like Byron and Keats, Shelley is in good measure an
important poet because he so fully realized that Wordsworth had decisively (in the modern phrase) raised his consciousness. Shelley fully
understood that Wordsworth had opened the possibility of representing
with an unparalleled intensity human experiences of natural phenomena,
thereby offering opportunities to discover the best ways in which
humankind could dwell in this world, how best we could act upon—and
be acted upon by—natural circumstances. That is why he presents
Wordsworth's political apostasy in *Peter Bell the Third* as the result—not
the cause—of Wordsworth's betrayal of his original naturalistic vision.

We can afford to be more charitable than Shelley toward Wordsworth.
We can recognize that probably the only nonreligious way of resolving his
contradictory dual vision of nature was through fully developed ecological
conceptions that he can scarcely be blamed for not attaining. Indeed, it
would not be absurd to say that ecological thinking developed in order to
make sense of the kind of paradoxical satisfaction articulated in the early
version of "The Ruined Cottage." We must also credit Wordsworth's
courage: very few of his successors beyond the second generation of
romantic poets were capable of even attempting the temporalized materialistic naturalism that informs the "The Ruined Cottage" and his other
superb early works, such as "Michael."

If we are honest, moreover, we will admit it is never easy in the course of
life to sustain the fundamental romantic view that the natural world is precious because it is vital, because it is always changing, so that individual
parts of it *must* suffer loss and destruction. It is not easy, for one reason,
because those who delight in this transformativeness expose themselves to

searing pains of consciousness to which those indifferent to natural circumstances are less vulnerable. The sufferings inflicted by natural process
are not only those undergone by Margaret; they are also those experienced
by the poet of "Tintern Abbey" as he tells us in "Surprised by Joy," a sonnet evoked by the death of his little daughter.

> Surprised by joy—impatient as the Wind
> I turned to share the transport—Oh! with whom
> But Thee, deep buried in the silent tomb,
> That spot which no vicissitude can find?
> Love, faithful love, recalled thee to my mind—
> But how could I forget thee? Through what power,
> Even for the least division of an hour,
> Have I been so beguiled as to be blind
> To my most grievous loss!—That thought's return
> Was the worst pang that sorrow ever bore,
> Save one, one only, when I stood forlorn,
> Knowing my heart's best treasure was no more;
> That neither present time, nor years unborn
> Could to my sight that heavenly face restore.
>
> (420)

The romantics' willingness to make themselves vulnerable to such anguish
arose from their refusal simply to oppose culture to nature. At their best they
were skeptical of claims that a divine origin and future personal redemption
distinguished mankind from all other natural beings. They also rejected,
however, philosophical commitments that would have led them toward
defining humankind by modes expressive of indifference to the physical actualities of natural life. Their poetry records struggles toward a more complicated understanding of how nature and culture may adapt to one another.
Their searching required that they not evade the contradiction so powerfully
epitomized in "A Slumber Did My Spirit Seal" and so painfully evoked in
"Surprised by Joy." That is why the highest attainment that the romantics can
imagine for a human being is a capacity to endure violently contradictory
emotions. Ambivalence must characterize the most intense experiences of
creatures at once natural and cultural, whose finest achievements necessarily
express awareness of the irresolvably dubious implications in that duality.

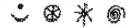

four

Poetic Ecosystems: Art for Nature's Sake

When I introduced the term *ecology* into romantic criticism twenty years ago, I coupled it with the term *holiness*, even though ecological views are naturalistic, not religious.[1] Ecological conceptions of natural reality need not exclude ideas or attitudes sometimes associated with religiosity, though they allow no place for any transcendent deity. This openness accounts for the attraction of ecological thought to some dim-witted and unpleasant mysticisms. The ecological tendencies of romantic poets, however, were more complex than mere substitutes for religious experiences. This complexity can be untangled by recognizing that, as I pointed out two decades ago, Wordsworth's most significant "nature poetry" is characterized by a conception of inclusive wholeness like that central to ecological thought. Such conceptions need not be driven by derogations of "spirit," even when, as in "Home at Grasmere," their focus is on physical, materialistic nature.

This so-called fragment (that I suggested is *The Recluse*, the great philosophic poem Wordsworth was unable to complete) was published only long after Wordsworth's death, and only in our own day has attracted the intensive critical attention it deserves. Commentators now recognize that "Home at Grasmere" contains perhaps Wordsworth's most significant statement of his artistic purposes in relation to the natural world, especially in the passage he printed as a "prospectus" to *The Excursion*.[2] The poem presents difficulties for some critics, however, because it so literally represents a natural locale, Grasmere Vale, as so numinous a "Dwelling-place." Wordsworth delineates the valley as complete in itself, deficient in no way,

> A Whole without dependence or defect,
> . . . Unity entire, . . .
>
> (168–69)

embodying the possibility of a truly integrated life that excludes no aspect of human potentiality, even for pain:

> Here may the heart
> Breathe in the air of fellow-suffering
> Dreadless . . .
>
> (448–50)

This plenitude is a function—paradoxically—of the Vale's limitedness. By dwelling within its "self-sufficing" wholeness the poet discovers total integration of psychic and physical being.

The logic of this claim lies in the poet's belief that if we can fully engage ourselves with what today would be called an ecosystem, we simultaneously escape two prisons. The first is what Shelley was to call the prison of immediate sensory impressions, the purely material environment that animals inhabit. The second prison is constructed by human ideational systems invented out of ignorance or distortion of nature's physical actualities. In the "Grasmere ecosystem" such intellectual falsifications are correctable through the grounding of sensory experience in conscious wholeness of being. Reciprocally, a complete consciousness is realizable through physical participation in the unity of the ecosystem. Full functioning of the poet's sensory, intellectual, and imaginative capacities give rise to the self-consciousness embodied in the poem itself of how the vale operates as a humanly enhancing, instead of limiting, environment.

This is why "Home at Grasmere" (like most of Wordsworth's finest poetry) is dominated by a rhetoric of repetition. To evoke in us a sense of the nurturing ecosystemic wholeness, the poet must continuously present overlapping or superimposed relationships and patterns of relationship. The superimpositions are especially necessary because any ecosystem's wholeness is temporal as well as spatial. An ecosystem is a constantly self-transforming continuity. No ecosystem exists outside of time or is adequately representable as anything other than an encompassing ongoing process made up of diversely intersecting subordinate temporal processes.

The intense pleasure of diverse present moments upon which "Home at Grasmere" focuses is created by interanimations of memories and prophetic intuitions. Representations of Wordsworth's immediate sensations are shot through with language both recollective and premonitory. The wholeness he celebrates demands that every immediate impression exists through its dynamic interdependence with what has preceded it and may succeed it. Because each sensation with which the vale "swarms" thus recalls and foretells others, no experience, even that of the poem's composition, is isolated or isolating, even though each experience is distinctively singular—as is the poem itself.

This is why Wordsworth represents the valley not only as a place "where solitude is not" but even more surprisingly as "A true Community," where "human and brute" are equally "undisturbed" possessors of a "Recess" that is equally "their legislative Hall, their Temple, and their glorious dwelling-place."[3] Thus wrenched from its context, this language may startle. The poem's purpose, however, is to represent how the conventionally antagonistic "cultural" and "natural" may in fact felicitously interanimate. Once we grant that these modes of being may not be merely antithetical, it is not absurd to read back into the phenomena of plant and animal existence equivalences of mankind's religious and legal aspirations. The vale's preciousness is that it facilitates reciprocity among "Dwellers" in their "dwelling-place," a "true community . . . of many into one incorporate" (819–20).

Determinative of this self-differentiated wholeness is Wordsworth's presentation of no feature of the ecosystem as more basic, more primary, either more "primitive" or more "privileged," than any other. The specific sights and sounds that delight him in the vale are only a part of its inclusively supportive character. How he is "received" by Grasmere Vale is as important as his perceptions of it; we are made conscious of the geographical locale as equally sustaining and sustained by social activities.

"Home at Grasmere" thus justifies the aptness of Alan Bewell's insistence upon Wordsworth's modifying of Enlightenment "anthropological" attitudes, for here we find the poet bringing close to himself (and so to his readers) natural features that had traditionally been regarded as marginal to supremely civilized life.[4]

Along with their subverting of conventional exoticism, Wordsworth's best poems refuse to accept any absolutely "objective" view—of other people or of natural phenomena. They simultaneously deny, however, that incomplete or "prejudiced" subjective experiences are less valuable than statements of philosophic principles or rational generalizations. This is why "Home at Grasmere" celebrates how all parts of human nature and physical nature interactively contribute to an inclusive vitality of being multiform but not hierarchized. The poem would have us imagine a coordinating continuity of sensations with thoughts that enables different individualities to exist as interdependencies. Yet the poem equally resists any leveling into simple equivalences. Each entity within the Grasmere ecosystem contributes in its own singular fashion to the successful totality: "Each Being has his office . . . all worthy" (880–81). The self-conscious poet is different from nonself-conscious creatures in the valley, with complex responsibilities imposed by his self-consciousness. That does not make him superior to the other beings with whom he dwells. Each has its place and its functions to establish the interrelated wholeness that is the true reality of "Grasmere Vale"—something more than a topographical entity—an integrated existence from which all elements through diverse reciprocities may profit and prosper.

This is the basis for Wordsworth's mind-staggering assurance that the grandest and most beautiful imaginings of human life may be realized in the "simple produce of the common day," by humans satisfied to be "nothing more than what we are." Critics have had difficulty recognizing the profound implications, cultural as well as ideological, of this Wordsworthian simplicity without simplification. The liberating power of realized interdependence of man and natural world provides, as I have already suggested, the ground for a peculiarly romantic conception of authentic individuality. Romantic individuality is a singleness incompatible with isolation. Essential to this perspective is the recognition of each specific element of the whole, not as equal to every other but as equally necessary in its special fashion to the integrity of the entire system.

⌣ ⊛ ✳ ◉

This conception of individuality is the bedrock of romantic politics.

Because the thrust of romantic poetry was oriented along these eco-logical-anthropological lines, it often found itself at odds with progres-sive, perfectibilitarian, reformist, or utopian political movements. Plain-ly enough, the author of "Home at Grasmere" could never have sub-scribed unqualifiedly to a doctrine of the "rights of man" abstracted from particular humans' specific physical conditions. He could never have regarded absolute equality as *the* solution to social difficulties. For the romantic poets, the (quite literally) infinite worth of each unique life, however small, insignificant, or humble, depended not on its being equal to others but, instead, on its making a peculiar contribution to the whole-ness of an entire system of vitality, a wholeness constituted by almost end-less differences of diversely individualized beings.

This bias explains the curious combination in the romantic poets of energetic, idealistic enthusiasms with tendencies toward quietistic atti-tudes of "wise passiveness." As Wordsworth proclaims in "Home at Gras-mere," a wonderfully fulfilling life is possible right now, right here, in a quiet existence (consisting, to be sure, of endless movement: "Who could look / And not feel motions there?") in a tiny locality on the familiar earth—if one can recognize the opportunities for participatory energies offered by nature. A falsification of one's true individuality, then, is like-ly to be induced by narrow ideological partisanship, and by demands for public acts to attain immediate, limited political objectives. Another counterforce to impassioned political activity arose from what might be called an anthropological (as distinct from a religious) forgivingness of spirit, a respect for the position of others founded in recognition that any vitally encompassing wholeness must be constituted of subordinate dif-ferentiations, even incompatibilities. Such a tendency was intensified in the romantics by their alertness to the historical dimensions of all living systems. That things have changed, are changing, will change, works against easy assurance that one specific political act will be of paramount importance.

The inconsistencies of romantic political attitudes are likely to appear vivid and glaring to a modern reader because the poets lacked the system-atized knowledge, and even appropriate vocabulary, necessary to articulate fully what today we can identify as an ecological understanding. To put the issue crudely, there was no possibility of the poets' developing a "green" politics, although that was a direction toward which the thrust of their thinking pointed them. The lack of supportive intellectual systematization for their ecological views, however, had the positive effect of turning them toward "imagination" as a central concept. The unity of an ecosystem, after all, is not something sensorily perceptible, even though it is determinative of our sensory experience. Nor is the entirety of the system readily definable in traditionally logical terms, even though reason is essential to our understanding of it. An ecosystem, finally, although very complicated, is also something very specific. So it is understandable that the romantics emphasized the importance of complex integral unities of being whose wholenesses could only be *imagined*. Such imagining, however, tends not to lead toward what we think of as a *realpolitik*.

If the proto-ecological tendencies of the romantic poets sometimes led them into what impress us today as ideological hesitancies and inconsistencies (inconsistencies perhaps foretelling some of the confusions of "green" politics in our own age), their imaginative naturalism could accommodate less contradictorily the religious attitudes of their era. English Anglicanism at the end of the eighteenth century (in contrast to the religious fanaticisms that had distinguished the previous century) was in some respects encouraging to a mixing of naturalism with the numinous. The national church in Wordsworth's youth was not yet strongly evangelical, reasonably tolerant, and capable of absorbing many Enlightenment ideas that a more fervent and zealous Christianity would have rejected. The church's prevailing deistical bias freed Wordsworth to explore in his experiences of the natural world what he could portray as "spiritual" qualities without feeling discomfort about his orthodoxy. During the first twenty years of his career as poet, he certainly appears to have been at ease in ignoring the central tenets of the church to which he belonged, while describing events specially noteworthy because of resonances they evoked that can only be described as spiritual. The poet assumes his readers will not find shocking a "religiosity" of natural experience. By and large, his assumption seems to have been justified; in the many vigorous attacks on his poetry in his own day, the charge of religious blasphemy remained a secondary feature.

Philosophically, of course, it was Spinoza who served as the chief intellectual support for the development of such proto-ecological views as Wordsworth espoused. Spinoza's role in all of romantic thought,

despite the work of scholars like Thomas McFarland, has been unduly slighted in most recent romantic criticism.[5] That role is admittedly difficult to assess, for the complexity of Spinoza's work lends itself to very contradictory kinds of interpretation. Coleridge, for example, though drawing heavily on Spinoza, whom he used, for instance, in his *natura naturans/natura naturata* distinction as defining the function of imagination, finally strained to refute what he saw as the atheistic results of Spinoza's pantheism. Indubitably Spinoza was seized upon by many thinkers desirous of eliminating any conception of God. Spinoza himself, however, rejected not God but God as a transcendent creator distinct from his creation.

Perhaps the most thoughtful of recent commentators has best summarized the simultaneous depth and complexity of Spinoza's contribution:

> His philosophical revolution anticipated major trends in European modernization, including secularization, Biblical criticism, the rise of natural science, the Enlightenment, and the liberal-democratic state. Above all, he put forward a radically new philosophical principle that I call the philosophy of immanence. It views this-worldly existence as all there is, as the only actual being and the sole source of ethical value. God himself is identical with the totality of nature.[6]

Spinoza's God-Nature, divine nature, is self-creating and self-created, acting according to the laws of its own being. This is the basis for Spinoza's denial of the existence of chance or contingency; everything in the cosmos is *determined,* in the sense that it manifests the processes of a continuously ongoing unified, comprehensive system. As Stuart Hampshire has pointed out, however, "This so-called pantheistic doctrine can in fact be fairly represented as the metaphysical expression of the ideal . . . of a unified science, that is, of a . . . science which would enable every natural change to be shown as a completely determined effect with a single system of causes."[7]

The potential relevance of this "scientific-religious" view to ecosystem thinking has been obscured by later and metaphysically cruder assertions of atheistic naturalism. Much "scientific atheism" runs counter to Spinoza's conception of eternally self-creating, infinitely complex natural orderings. Jacques Monod, the Nobel prize–winning biochemist, states the position of such modern atheists with admirable clarity: "The universe was not pregnant with life nor the biosphere with man. Our number came up in the Monte Carlo game."[8] This view, although founded on the valid perception that chance is at the heart of all contemporary biological thinking, contravenes more ecologically oriented Darwinists and Lamarckians, as is suggested by Monod's later assertion in *Chance and Necessity* that mankind must awake from "his millenary dream and discover his total solitude, his fundamental isolation. He must realize that, like a gypsy, he lives on the boundary of an alien world; a world that is deaf to his music, and as indifferent to his hopes as it is to his suffering or his crimes" (159). It would be difficult to find a statement more antithetical than Monod's either to Spinozistic immanence or to Wordsworth's proto-ecological view of man as truly at home only in the natural world. For Spinoza and Wordsworth, a person is deluded who regards him- or herself as existing in "fundamental isolation." It is precisely the thrust of romantic ecological thought to conceive of *all* things, including humankind, as nourishingly interrelated within natural systems.

Monodian existentialism, like a good deal of post-Darwinian thought that claims evolutionary ideas as the ground for affirming humankind's alienated condition, in one significant respect weirdly misrepresents Darwin. These existentialists ignore exactly the assertions that brought down upon Darwin the harshest condemnations of the conventionally pious in his own day, for example, his observation that "the difference in mind between man and the higher animals, great as it is, certainly is one of degree and not of kind."[9]

Exactly what made Darwinianism anathema to orthodox Victorians— that it showed man inescapably linked to, rather than separable from, the processes of nature—has also, paradoxically, made his fundamental position as unacceptable to modern "cultural critics" who disregard every society's foundation in physical nature. Ecological thinking follows Darwin more rigorously in challenging all presuppositions of humankind's separateness from the natural world—whether through the work of a transcendent deity or the supposedly alienating work of self-conscious cultural structures. Spinoza, of course, knew nothing of evolution, but he did argue that humankind could be conceived as capable of participating happily and organizedly within (not existing in inescapable separateness from) self-creating, self-sustaining systems of nature. The scholars who

have discerned and described the enormous importance of Spinozistic thought at the end of the eighteenth century have, sometimes inadvertently, depicted one of the cradles of ecology, a significant symptom of which is the frequency with which Spinozism was contradictorily condemned as pantheistic and atheistic.

It is illuminating, finally, to scrutinize the nonexclusiveness of the ecological tendencies in Wordsworth's poetry from the perspective of postromantic aesthetic history. From that angle, what is most amazing about Wordsworth is his innocence of any commitment to art for art's sake. Wordsworth dedicated his life to being a poet and nothing else. He readily sacrificed anything and anybody (particularly the women around him) to his chosen pursuit. He was a skilled and conscientious craftsman, dedicatedly attentive to every aspect of his art; and no one believed more passionately than he in the importance of poetry. But not for its own sake; not as an aesthetic accomplishment segregated from the rest of social—or natural—life. Wordsworth's poetic program was the antithesis of the later nineteenth-century aesthetes'. The kind of attitude that led to Wallace Stevens's idea of art as a supreme fiction is, finally, foreign to Wordsworth's ecological-anthropological enterprise.

This dedication to one's art without defining oneself in opposition to the natural world on either religious or aesthetic grounds is carried forward by Shelley and Byron, and even influenced Keats, the first of the major nineteenth-century poets to move toward segregating poetry into a distinct realm of "the aesthetic." Obvious as is romantic poetry's fundamental hostility to "pure" aestheticism, attention to that hostility brightly illumines the strength of the poets' ecological orientation. Ecology urges us to recognize the value of comprehending interrelationships among all forms of life—including humankind—to one another and to inanimate portions of their environment. Ecological thinking insists that we be steadily conscious of living in a real natural world with which we meaningfully interact and in which our actions have discernibly specific consequences. An ecological vision, then, is one that assumes that all human beings bear profound responsibilities toward others, not just other humans, but other life forms—along with their and our habitat. That we exist not in elitist isolation but interdependently is a conviction that imposes concrete and difficult ethical burdens—a prime reason why ecologically oriented poetry must resonate with moral if not spiritual overtones.

Perhaps the most provocative expression of the moral difficulties of a proto-ecological attitude appears in Wordsworth's poem "Nutting." Critics have observed that the story the poet tells of his expedition in search of hazelnuts, costumed in unnecessarily ragged "nutting clothes," is an account of a rape. This true observation has led to elaborate psychological interpretations obliterating the literal circumstances detailed in the poem. Some of these are worth recovering, if only to give a deeper understanding of the forces in the poem encouraging modern psychological analyses.[10]

For example, the clothing with which the young Wordsworth so ostentatiously armors himself against natural hazards manifests an almost military preparedness for his "sallying forth." He is garbed for "forcing" his way through nature, reminding us of the younger Wordsworth of "Tintern Abbey" who was more like one "flying from something that he dreads, than one / Who sought the thing he loved." The conventionality of this readiness to fight nature is exposed by lovely hazel nook, whose pristine charm is realized through linguistic negatives, "unvisited," and with "not a broken bough," proving that the self-protection "more . . . than need was" reveals young Wordsworth truly unprepared for the beneficence of nature.

Not bringing to the grove a "heart that watches and receives," the boy could not feel for long the enchantment of the idyllic coppice. He does bring, however, a heart capable of briefly luxuriating in the unspoiled sensual seductiveness of the "virgin scene," lying with his cheek on a mossy rock listening to the "murmur and murmuring sound" of the "fairy water breaks" of the gentle stream. Then, abruptly, he leaps up and ravages the grove, dragging "to earth both branch and bough" so that the mossy bower is "deformed and sullied." Indubitably the poem's language suggests sexual violation as it displays the destructively aggressive effects already implicit in the boy's costuming of himself. Yet the poem would not be so unusual were these suggestions not so firmly embedded within an account of the destruction of a part of the natural world, of a hazel grove.

Rape—alas—is not an unfamiliar topic in European poetry. But I know of no poem before "Nutting" that centers on the shame of an individual's careless ravaging of the natural environment. The destruction the young poet suddenly wreaks, therefore, is perhaps both more significantly gratuitous and more self-contradictory than an actual rape. That it is a

grove of trees that the boy despoils facilitates the older poet's judgment on the power of aggressive impulses embodied in his admission that he may have turned "from the mutilated bower" not with "a sense of pain," but perhaps feeling satisfied or even exulting.

The uncertainty of superimposed perspectives that runs throughout the poem is possible because it is "only" a hazel grove that the young poet ravaged. The depth of contemporary sexualized readings of "Nutting," that is to say, is made possible by the poem's articulating sexual suggestiveness through a reminiscence of abominable behavior toward the external natural world, toward trees. The boy's first delight in the bower, for example, is described from the perspective of more mature experience, as appears in such comments as

> A temper known to those, who, after long
> And weary expectation have been blest
> With sudden happiness beyond all hope.
> (26–28)

This doubled perspective becomes crucial at the conclusion of the incident, because it enables Wordsworth to affirm the need to overcome narcissistic pseudoinnocence with a self-awareness deriving from a contemplating of experience.

The disclaimer of lines 48–49, "unless I now / Confound my present feelings with the past," reminds us that the poet is a different person from the one who ravaged the bower. There remains the suggestion, however, that the boy may have experienced something that the older man rightly identifies as pain. In *composing* his poem, the poet's lost feelings may have been recovered. Then at this uncertain crux we are presented with a second narrative ellipsis in the unexpected turn to the "maiden":

> Then, dearest Maiden, move along these shades
> In gentleness of heart; with gentle hand
> Touch—for there is a spirit in the woods.
> (53–55)

These concluding lines may be read as an address to the feminine self within the poet, as an exhortation to himself to keep faith with a true innocence that—paradoxically—he has acquired, through meditating on the effects of his pseudoinnocent destructive act. In this view, the poem treats of a reconstruction of personality, a reshaping of self to become capable of respecting and cherishing external nature. By addressing the feminine component within himself, the poet enacts his poem's message: only through intense self-awareness (powerful enough to challenge a man's sense of his own masculinity) can we escape the destructiveness of a narcissism fostered by assumptions that we must "attack" and "defend" ourselves against our environment.

Yet such connecting of phases of the poet's own being is but one span of interrelationships that this deceptively simple-seeming poem dramatizes. It is only after the boy has mutilated the bower, when the "murmuring sound" has been silenced, when the nook has "patiently" surrendered "its quiet being," that the livingness of the natural scene is fully realized—for the boy, for the poet, and for the reader. Only when faced with "silent trees" does the delicate yet vital relation between human being and hazel grove appear in all its combined potency and fragility. It was easy for the boy to ravage the beauty of the grove. Yet even when destroyed, that beauty persists in its poignantly affecting silence—which the poet has articulated not just to himself but also to his sister—and to us.

That the poem should be made into an address to a "Maiden," therefore, is peculiarly appropriate, insofar as Wordsworth has described a cultural attack on nature, embodying the violence hidden within that ambiguous creature, a "nature lover." The ambivalence thus represented by the upsetting of the conventional conception of nature as feminine is reinforced by the dubiety of the poet's memory. The admonition to the Maiden arises from the poet's present sense of the evil he did as something he may not have experienced at the moment he looked back at the despoiled grove: in that retrospect he may not then have "felt a sense of pain." Even if he did, at the earlier time he could not have understood what he now does in composing the poem questioning the entire story of his behavior. The compositional act brings to light the potential destructiveness within his early passionate responsiveness to the natural world. It is only with the writing of the poem, or, better, after having written the poem, that he (and through him the reader) is able to imagine "a spirit in the woods."

However one interprets that ungendered "spirit in the woods," it is a spirit created by the poet's contemplation of his violation of a natural scene. Wordsworth's "spirit" evokes a feeling for a quality in the natural world—not in ourselves—to which we ought to learn to relate more responsibly than the poet did as boy. The damage that we do to our environment, the diminishments we work on its capacity for healing and nourishing us, he shows to be not solely the product of thoughtless exploiters of natural resources. The spirit in the woods may be violated even by those capable of responding intensely to nature's sensual pleasures. Even the Maiden must learn to "move along these shades / In gentleness of heart."

This kind of reading in no way dismisses the purely psychosexual interpretations that have dominated our criticism for two generations. But if we admit that "Nutting" is first and literally about our relations to the natural world, we will recognize that the poem foregrounds powerful and difficult ethical choices that may be obscured by psychologically universalizing interpretations. Because Wordsworth's proto-ecological view of the natural world is necessarily complex and holistic, such choices inevitably call to mind ideas about behavior that connect, if only tangentially, to feelings and attitudes that historically have usually been associated with religious experiences and religious ideals. In Wordsworth's poem, however, these resonances are made entirely immanent, are embedded completely in the sensory experience of the material world of nature. Romantic Wordsworth (and in this Byron and Shelley closely follow his lead) represents his claim to being a poet as involving him (and through him his readers) in direct responsibilities to more than himself and more than his art—including his and their natural environment.

The romantics' sense of responsibility to nature as central to their being socially valuable poets poses difficult issues of responsibility for their critics. Contemporary critics have preferred to dwell on the poets' ideological shortcomings or personality quirks rather than to inquire into the social responsibilities of their profession.[11] As I survey the immense body of recent criticism of "Nutting," I am troubled by the consistent omission from it of serious concern for the literal circumstances, both of the young poet in the hazel grove and of the older poet's writing of his experience there, circumstances that seem to have been of enormous importance to Wordsworth. It is not that all the talk of phallic oedipal-ism, maternal discourse, and the like is nonsensical. There is something skewed, however, in recent criticism's reluctance to admit how the literal story of the poem raises profound questions about our relation to our physical environment, questions that appear to have played a decisive part in Wordsworth's writing of the poem. To pass over these questions, to deny the significance of the "literalness" of the hazel grove in pursuing our fascination with politics or personal sexual psychology, is to make manifest a specific (if unstated) judgment about the value of literature and the criticism of literature that seems fundamentally at odds with the poet's own valuations. By denying the importance of external nature in poems such as "Nutting," moreover, contemporary critics, while freeing themselves to explore interesting matters of ideology or private psychology, implicitly define both poetry and criticism as socially trivial.

Far more profoundly than we have been willing to admit, literary criticism of the past half-century, even that pretending to ideological orientations, has surreptitiously accepted as unarguably given the nihilistic implications of a commitment to art for art's sake only. Our literary criticism now *assumes* the effective isolation of the aesthetic realm, a realm of philosophic or psychological universalizing insulated from any practical significance to our society's practical development. A good way to begin restoring the usefulness of criticism, instead of insisting that all critics adopt some politically correct ideological position, would be simply to suppose that the kind of self-exploration that poetry such as "Nutting" can foster might help us to identify beneficial and dangerous relations between human beings and our natural environment. For it is on the health of the natural world that all ideologies, all societies, and all cultures ultimately depend.

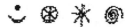

five

Discovering Nature's Voice

This chapter describes how ecologically slanted nature poetry came into being and how it evolved in the romantic era.

In the first edition of *Lyrical Ballads* in 1798 the first poem by Wordsworth is burdened with his longest title, "Lines Left upon a Seat in a Yew-Tree, which Stands near the Lake of Esthewaite, on a Desolate Part of the Shore, yet Commanding a Beautiful Prospect." This is followed immediately by his co-author's "The Nightingale: A Conversation Poem." The sequence is especially appropriate if, as some think, parts of the last lines of Wordsworth's poem were written by Coleridge. Be that as it may, the subtitle of Coleridge's poem identifies it as a new kind of lyric, a "conversation" poem, which in theme and metrical form parallels the new kind of inscription poem embodied in "Lines Left upon a Seat."

This conjunction is interesting because very soon Coleridge was to turn against what he came to call Wordsworth's pantheism and to give up writing "conversation" poems. Coleridge went on to devote major energies of his long intellectual career to defending a transcendental vision of divinity hostile to romantic proto-ecological nature poetry and, significantly, to the writing of very little poetry of any kind. But at the height of his intimacy with Wordsworth, Coleridge composed poems as ecologically oriented as his friend's.

Geoffrey Hartman has convincingly marshaled evidence showing how Wordsworth's lyric grows out of a synthesizing transformation of several conventions of nature-inscription poetry.[1] Wordsworth changed the character of these genres by allowing natural scenes, as Hartman puts it, to "speak" to readers directly, instead of presenting scenes overlaid by allegorical or other elaborate rhetorical devices. The reversal was worked by the poet's synthesizing of several interrelated generic traditions. "Lines Left upon a Seat" marks the breakthrough point at which a distinctive new form emerges out of the combining of epigram (this source suggested by the cumbersome title), the nature inscription, and the votive epitaph—which distinguished the genus loci, the divine spirit, of a particular place. Each of these genres conventionally used rhyme. Like Coleridge in his conversation poem, Wordsworth in his new kind of nature poetry replaces rhyme with blank verse. This "opening" of form helped him to dissolve the boundary between poet and natural world that had been emphasized by elaborate artifices in epigrammatic and epitaphic verse. Wordsworth and landscape, instead, speak in dialogue "more naturally." In Wordsworth's lyric, describing is literally transformed into inscribing—which justifies the pretense in poems such as "Tintern Abbey" and "Mont Blanc" that the lines we read were literally written down at the site from which the landscape described was viewed, as if a conversation were being recorded as it occurred.

These formal innovations facilitate representation of the poet's individualized interactions with nature. The place where the yew seat itself is found is "desolate," but the vista from it is lovely. The loneliness of setting in which the poem is inscribed is stressed by negations: it is without "sparkling rivulet" or "verdant herb," the "barren boughs" unvisited by bees.

> Yet, if the wind breathe soft, the curling waves,
> That break against the shore, shall lull thy mind
> By one soft impulse saved from vacancy.[2]

The personifications characteristic of the earlier forms here diffuse into a "speaking" landscape—by means of the "pathetic fallacy" of attributing to natural phenomena human intentions and feelings. So the wind "breathes" and the waves "lull, thus "saving" by "one soft impulse" the mind "from vacancy."

The lyric itself embodies, then, the capacity to feel natural processes as if they were humanized events, and this enables the mind to be filled by a lively wealth of pleasing sensations. The Wordsworthian nature poem thus inverts the elegiac mode dominant in the epitaphic and inscriptive forms it quietly but radically transfigures. Though a memorial of the man, "of no common soul" who built the seat that contains the verses, Wordsworth's "Lines" present him as a negative model, ruined by gloomy narcissism. His self-injuring melancholy was induced by the world's "neglect" of his unusual aspirations and capabilities. Indignant at being ignored, he pridefully withdrew into himself. At this spot he "a morbid pleasure nourished" in tracing in the barren scene an "emblem" of his unfruitful life. Or, raising his eyes, he would contemplate the lovely distant scene—

> and he would gaze till it became
> Far lovelier, and his heart could not sustain
> The beauty, still more beauteous!

Thus feeding his fancy on "visionary views" he died unprofitably.

His fate should warn us that "pride / Howe'er disguised in its own majesty / Is littleness" and that he

> who feels contempt
> For any living thing, hath faculties
> Which he has never used.
>
> (40)

The living being upon whom the inscriber exercised contempt was himself. The verses tell of a moral suicide brought about through a failure of the victim to allow himself to respond to the healing influence offered by his natural environment, here identified with an interplaying of beauty and barrenness. In the final lines, perhaps partly composed by Coleridge, the moral is made explicit, condemning "the man whose eye / Is ever on himself" as one looking on "the least of Nature's works." It is further asserted not only that "true knowledge leads to love" but also that "true dignity" abides with the man who "can still suspect, and still revere himself."

Though the least of nature's works, and appropriately self-suspicious, a human being should never become self-contemptuous. An enormous number of romantic poems focus on this issue, how to retain self-reverence even while skeptically scrutinizing our impulses and motivations, since we are all adept at self-betrayal. The fundamental solution is suggested by these early "Lines" of Wordsworth: recognize oneself not as an isolated being but as one fully existent only insofar as reciprocally interacting with one's environment. The healthy response to neglect is not withdrawal into prideful egoism, for that is separative, death-oriented. I may be the least of beings, but nonetheless evidence of my worthiness is afforded by the pleasure to be found in bestowing my humanness— which means exercising my self-awareness, entering it into the interactivity of an ecosystem's operations—on other elements in my environment. I can so function if I but realize that I possess a place not defined solely by my social circumstances within the beautiful-barren world of nature. Implicit in this view is a powerful if unusual politics: the most trivial, commonplace, unnoticed of persons is naturally deserving of respect as an individual. That is *the* fundamental romantic political commitment. It is founded on the conviction that we are not alienated, unless through morbid narcissism we alienate ourselves and lose the wealth of gentle sensations to be experienced in processes of full reciprocity with our natural habitat.

Coleridge's "The Nightingale" develops the softness and implicit yieldingness of Wordsworth's lyric more explicitly and affirmatively through what might be called a poetics of completely felt negations. The profoundest fashion in which it transfigures its lyric tradition, however, appears only through its contrast with Coleridge's parallel poem composed just three years earlier and reprinted two years previously under the title "To the Nightingale."

> Sister of love-lorn Poets, Philomel!
> How many Bards in city garret pent,
> While at their window they with downward eye
> Mark the faint lamp-beam on the kennell'd mud,
> And listen to the drowsy cry of Watchmen
> (Those hoarse unfeather'd Nightingales of Time!),

How many wretched Bards address *thy* name,
And hers, the full-orbed Queen that shines above.
But I *do* hear thee, and the high bough mark,
Within whose mild moon-mellow'd foliage hid
Thou warblest sad thy pity-pleading strains.
Oh! I have listen'd, till my working soul,
Waked by those strains to thousand phantasies,
Absorb'd hath ceas'd to listen! Therefore oft,
I hymn thy name: and with a proud delight
Oft will I tell thee, Minstrel of the Moon!
"Most musical, most melancholy" Bird!
That all thy soft diversities of tone,
Tho' sweeter far than the delicious airs
That vibrate from a white-arm'd Lady's harp,
What time the languishment of lonely love
Melts in her eye, and heaves her breast of snow,
Are not so sweet as is the voice of her,
My Sara—best beloved of human kind!
When breathing the pure soul of tenderness,
She thrills me with the Husband's promis'd name![3]

Here the poet contrasts his situation of actually hearing the bird singing above him with that of garret-penned poets looking down into "kennel-l'd mud." These depend on their fancies nourished in a purely literary tradition, whose conventionalities are dramatized by an urban environment foretelling T. S. Eliot's "Preludes." Yet Coleridge portrays the actuality of his different rural experience in as rigidly conventionalized terms. The bird he hears, for instance, is Philomela, presented as definitively described by Milton's line in "Il Penseroso."

Two years later in the 1798 "The Nightingale," however, Milton's line is remembered only to be dismissed as an "idle" thought.

And hark! the Nightingale begins its song,
"Most musical, most melancholy" Bird!
A melancholy Bird? O idle thought!
In nature there is nothing melancholy.
—But some night-wandering Man, whose heart was pierc'd

With the remembrance of a grievous wrong,
Or slow distemper or neglected love,
(And so poor Wretch! fill'd all things with himself
And made all gentle sounds tell back the tale
Of his own sorrows) he and such as he
First nam'd these notes a melancholy strain;
And many a poet echoes the conceit, . . .

(41.11–22)[4]

Coleridge was uncomfortably self-conscious about his subversion of Milton (and his earlier self) here and in an unconvincing footnote in the original *Lyrical Ballads* defended himself against a fancied charge of having "alluded with levity to a line in Milton" by claiming there was *dramatic* propriety in Milton's melancholy man so speaking of the bird. But Coleridge's drastic revision of the Miltonic tradition is even further developed as the poem progresses.

Rather than echo literary conceits, a true poet, he tells us

to the influxes
Of shapes and sounds and shifting elements
Surrendering his whole spirit

can with his song "make all nature lovelier, and itself / Be lov'd, like nature!" (27–34).

Yet in his epoch, Coleridge laments, conventionalized preconceptions, not real experience of nature, dominate "poetic" imagining:

And youths and maidens most poetical
Who lose the deep'ning twilights of the spring
In ball-rooms and hot theatres, they still
Full of meek sympathy must heave their sighs
O'er Philomela's pity-pleading strains.

(35–39)

This phrasing, which enacts the banality it condemns, mocks Coleridge's own earlier use of "pity-pleading strains," for he and his friends have, he tells us, learned a different lore—that "in Nature there is nothing melan-

choly," that "Nature's sweet voices" are "always full of love / And joyance!" The refutation of the Miltonic tradition is reinforced by the subtle movement into naturalistic accuracy as Coleridge identifies the "merry Nightingale" as male, not female. In these passages Coleridge contravenes his later theorizing by following Wordsworth into intriguing psychological complexities of experiential receptivity and projection. This poem warns that one distorts the truths of natural being when one projects into external nature narcissistic feelings. Yet one appreciates (and if a poet one can make manifest) the joyfulness and healing qualities offered to us by nature if we bestow upon it our finest human feelings. "The Nightingale" explains the seeming contradiction in sound Wordsworthian fashion, claiming that what one beneficently gives is in fact a return of what one has already received from natural phenomena by attending and attuning oneself to their most subtle and life-enhancing qualities.

Ecological thinking encourages the view that this Wordsworthian reciprocity need be no mere verbal trick. Any ecosystem works because individual contributions to its functioning are made by particular elements that can so contribute only because they belong to, are the creatures of, the encompassing system they help to constitute. Wordsworthian reciprocity points toward processes like that of "reentry" by which biologists like Edelman describe continuously modifying interactions between a human mind and the environment it explores (see chapter 9).

The extraordinary opening of "The Nightingale" allows us to understand such reciprocal processes, because the poem gives such a distinctive voice to what is apparently negated within the natural scene. The lyric begins with entirely absent features, no cloud, no slip of light, no colors. On the mossed bridge, artifact renaturalized over time, one senses the glimmer of the stream beneath but hears no sound of its flowing. The glimmer is echoed in the dimness of the stars, in which "we shall find / A Pleasure" recalling the effects of "vernal showers." Many eighteenth-century poets (even Coleridge in his "Lines: On an Autumnal Evening" of 1796) had written of evening, but none had evoked this soft, moist, blurrily diffused atmosphere of duskiness. The dim-gleaming twilight dramatizes the joyfulness the "merry Nightingale" pours forth, flooding the dusk with the "fast thick warble" of the "delicious notes" of "His love-chant."

On this cataract of joyous sound we are carried into the story of the deserted castle, "which the great lord inhabits not," visited by a "most gentle Maid"—"like a Lady vowed and dedicate / To something more than nature"—to hear the multitude of nightingales that burst forth with "skirmish and capricious passagings" in choral minstrelsy, like a strong wind sweeping through a hundred harps, where she has seen

> Many a nightingale perch giddily
> On blossomy twig still swinging from the breeze,
> And to that motion tune his wanton song
> Like tipsy Joy that reels with tossing head.
>
> (83–86)

This drunken wantonness of pleasure, by recalling "L'Allegro" instead of "Il Penseroso," reinforces Coleridge's reversing of the Miltonic attitude toward nature. The revision includes some subversive echoing of *Comus*, perhaps most subtly in the *comparison* of the Maid to a religious Lady. This surrounds the girl with connotations of purity and devoutness, even though what she seeks to witness at the abandoned estate is an orgy of "wanton song."

This justification for the denial that there is anything melancholy in nature is then confirmed by the concluding tale of the poet's infant son.

> once when he awoke
> In most distressful mood (some inward pain
> Had made up that strange thing, an infant's dream)
> I hurried with him to our orchard plot,
> And he beheld the moon, and hush'd at once
> Suspends his sobs, and laughs most silently,
> While his fair eyes that swam with undropt tears
> Did glitter in the yellow moon-beam! Well—
> It is a father's tale. But if that Heaven
> Should give me life, his childhood shall grow up
> Familiar with these songs, that with the night
> He may associate Joy!
>
> (98–109)

Coleridge returns to the quiet balminess of the opening, now transforming the glimmering moistness of the scene into the silent laughter of his

child, whose undropped tears glitter in the light of the moon, the vision of which has hushed his weeping. Then with the phrase that perhaps best justifies calling the lyric "a conversation poem," "Well!—It is a father's tale," Coleridge recovers in expanded form the sociality that is the human context making possible his perception of the joyance endemic to the natural world. There is more than *Comus*-contrastive sexual connotations in the poem's associating of joy with night, even as it is the absence of light that evoked the friendly conversing that the poem pretends to be. These verses invert extended conventions linking daylight with goodness and health in contrast to mystery and fear associated with the dark. Rejected is not only Milton's nightingale and the chaste heroine of *Comus* but even his representation of Satan as "darkness visible." We need not so divide nature, as Descartes divided mind and body. There is joy in *all* of nature for us, can we liberate ourselves from self-narrowing preconceptions. Our morbid fear of darkness (which in fact, as Shelley liked to emphasize, makes possible the special beauty of moon and stars and night birds' songs) is a narcissistic self-alienating that willfully blocks the enjoyment offered even by nature's seeming negativities.

This gently beautiful poem, as I have remarked, stands in contrast to Coleridge's usual un-Wordsworthian insistence that the One life within us and abroad originates entirely within the divine human soul, not in an interactive dialogue between man and nature. More typical of Coleridge is the poignant lament in "Dejection: An Ode," and his discomfort with his overt Wordsworthianism of "The Nightingale" probably helps to explain his derogation of the poem when he sent it to his friend.[5] But however rare in Coleridge's canon, the poem illustrates how the romantics' self-consciousness about their experience of the natural world necessitated their reshapings of literary forms and conventions. Coleridge's poem, furthermore, lays the ground for understanding the process by which such formal innovations were themselves productively retransformed by younger romantic poets.

Keats's "Ode to a Nightingale" plainly enough was written with Coleridge's poem in mind, and the ode's superiority derives in good measure from Keats's complex restructuring and reorienting of his predecessor's techniques and purposes.[6] His poem is neither a conversation poem nor an inscription in blank verse. It is a rhymed ode, traditionally the most formal of lyrics. True to the conventions of his form, Keats constantly moves beyond his immediate situation into the realms of myth and literary tradition, from blushful Hippocrene and personified moon with all her "fays" to Ruth and emperor and clown.

Yet Keats's nightingale sings a Coleridgean rather than a Miltonic strain, not in melancholy but in ecstatic happiness. Keats begins, indeed, by presenting himself as overly joyous in his response, "too happy in thine happiness." He quickly moves away, however, from the Wordsworthian-Coleridgean softness, gentleness, and negativity toward immediate intensities and absoluteness of sensation and imagination. The darkness where he sits, significantly, is complete—without the glimmering dimness so distinctive in Coleridge's poem. Not surprisingly, then, the ode evolves not toward the tumult of the flocking birds observed by gentle maiden, or a father's tale of his dream-distressed son, but, instead, into private imagining, a personal isolation that increasingly *contrasts* bird and poet to evoke the poignancy of the poet's, and all humanity's, isolation by self-consciousness from the joyousness of natural being.

The process here by which poetic tradition is reshaped is, to me at any rate, fascinating. For Keats begins from the Coleridgean position to develop the idea that melancholy, while not "in" nature, is simultaneously not the mere subjective fancy of a "distempered" man. Sorrow enters into the world with a human being's recognition of his separation from natural joyousness through the self-awareness that distinguishes him as human. By not attributing his sorrow to the bird, Keats dramatizes tragic implications in human self-consciousness. It is not only the pressures of Malthusian "hungry generations" that oppress us but even our creative imaginative powers. For these enable us to envision what the bird can never know, not merely our physical death, "to thy high requiem become a sod," but even the failure of the imagination's highest accomplishments to establish enduring ground for our intense delights, since it can finally only return us to the forlorn isolation of a "sole self." The ode thus inverts the Coleridgean position without denying the joyousness of nature.

So the inversion is not a symmetrical return to pre-Coleridgean attitudes. Although Keats might qualify as a youth "most poetical," in fact his relation to his heritage from the older romantics is intricately ambivalent, especially in regard to their ecological tendencies.[7] The nature of that intricacy appears in Keats's preference for a formalized, rhyming ode rather than a blank verse lyric. Yet his odic form has no exact precedent,

and his use of traditional themes, motifs, and images is original. Ruth had never before been associated with the nightingale, for instance, and the "emperor and clown" anticipate Yeats. Keats genuinely transfigures the traditions he inherits, which is why his poetry has had so much influence on subsequent writers. The source of that power is conspicuous in "An Ode to a Nightingale," because the poem so precisely articulates the theme of humanity's self-consciousness as separative from the world of nature, a decisive presupposition of most postromantic poetry.

The clarity of this foreshadowing obscures, however, the intensity of Keats's ambivalence both toward his own aspirations and toward the inspiration of his immediate predecessors—ambivalences more affectingly shaped in "To Autumn," composed some months later than the "Ode to a Nightingale" and its companion odes of May 1819. Though keeping to the generic form of these poems, "To Autumn" was never identified by Keats as an ode. What difference did he thus signal by this "omission" in title? In the autumnal non-ode the absolute opposition of conscious poet and joyously unself-conscious nightingale, "immortal" because unself-conscious, dissolves into a subtler articulation of the emotional tone of the mortality inherent in all natural being. Here the self-aware poet, the "I," disappears into a "viewless" realizing voice, formed by the natural processes it describes/inscribes, articulating a fulfillment-dissolution that carries to a new perceptual plane the spirit of early Wordsworthian engagement with nature. "To Autumn," in fact, might be read as a confirmatory gloss on Coleridge's claim for an absence of melancholy in the natural world—even in its seasonal diminishment. Here, perhaps with less interference than in any of his predecessor's poems, Keats enables the natural world with perfect ease to speak (even to sing) for and of itself. The poignancy of passing is thus tempered by an untroubled rendering of inexorable continuities of natural process admired as the lovely enchantment of change.

The success of "To Autumn" arises from the concreteness with which it represents the transitory fullness of the season in itself, admitting only to dismiss conventional comparisons with other parts of the year, rendering purely the thing in itself, even though the "thing" is of so diversely self-transforming an ensemble as a "season." There no poem in our language that so faithfully as "To Autumn" orchestrates the mutable tonalities of what I call ecological vision, a vision of cultured humankind with its imaginings as an integral part of a natural scene, in which "works and days," humanizing ritual and nonhuman natural process in both expansion and diminishment, are "felt in the blood and felt along the heart," so that even the passing through fulfillment of natural loveliness becomes transfigured into the enduring beauty of a singular linguistic expression.

My discussion in chapters 6 and 7 will suggest that "To Autumn" is probably closer to the central thrust of Keats's deepest thinking about the natural world and man's relation to it than his "Ode to a Nightingale." Yet I want to reemphasize here the clarity with which the ode foretells antiecological tendencies in later poetry and criticism, most notably in the development at the end of the nineteenth century of art-for-art's-sake aesthetics. That clarity, in the first place, highlights the fragility of the romantic proto-ecological position. In the work of the youngest of the canonical poets (although also the first to die) one sees already the influence of social, political, and intellectual pressures that were to overwhelm romantic ecological aspirations. This perception enables us to understand Keatsian ambivalence about humankind's place in nature not as a sign of weakness or indecisiveness but, to the contrary, as a positive fulfillment of a Wordsworthian (and consciously anti-Coleridgean) impulse in romantic poetry, an achievement aptly identified by Keats's celebrated phrase "negative capability."

"Negative capability" for Keats is possible only for those who can make discoveries for themselves; those who, because not trapped in preconceptions, are strong enough to face cheerfully the uncertainty of undefined alternatives and unrealized possibilities. In writing of negative capability, besides distinguishing himself from Coleridge, Keats seems to intuit with singular acuteness a peculiar quality in Wordsworth's contrastive genius.[8] The genius of the young Wordsworth was to discover for himself, to be wonderfully open to what impinged on him despite screens of conventionalized preconceptions. It was the hardening into a rigid didacticism of this capability to discover and not merely invent that rendered his later verse so disappointing. The failure of Wordsworth's openness to discovery had to be particularly distressing to Keats, who, through his social vulnerabilities, was always more threatened by pressures to accept, conform, and repeat the secured wisdom of others. These vulnerabilities were intensified by the generosity, even naïveté, of his responsiveness to the emotional power and enchanting beauty of the poetry of his predecessors.

Much have I travell'd in the realms of gold,
And many goodly states and kingdoms seen;
Round many western islands have I been
Which bards in fealty to Apollo hold.
Oft of one wide expanse had I been told
That deep-brow'd Homer ruled as his demesne;
Yet did I never breathe its pure serene
Till I heard Chapman speak out loud and bold:
Then felt I like some watcher of the skies
When a new planet swims into his ken;
Or like stout Cortez when with eagle eyes
He star'd at the Pacific—and all his men
Look'd at each other with a wild surmise—
Silent, upon a peak in Darien.

(64)

This is rightly the earliest of Keats's poems to be widely admired and praised, for it conveys the wonder of genuine discovery that is essential to all his finest verse. Few poets possess the wealth of enthusiasm so easily to confess their dependence on a translation, and fewer to admit a personal revelation arising from familiar, even conventional material. Yet the truth, which we mostly choose not to admit, is that usually we do read the great Greek poets in translation and are excited by works of which we have "oft been told." The surprisingly singular achievement of Keats's sonnet lies in its evoking the discovery not of the unknown but of the known, recovering the wonder of what has become familiar.

The "watcher of the skies," after all, is looking for the "new planet" that swims into his ken, as "stout Cortez" (a.k.a. Balboa) was seeking the Pacific. It is Cortez's feelings that image Keats's feelings—contrastively Cortez's followers "gaze at one another," not the Pacific, "in a wild surmise." The poet's personal identification with the explorer is crucial, because the sonnet is primarily not about the Homeric epics but about Keats's response to them. Of course the potency of his experience reflects glory on Chapman and Homer, but the primary wonder evoked is that of the respondent, the observer, the experiencer. The evocation of the literary experience, however, is through metaphors of imagined visions of natural phenomena, a planet, the Pacific ocean.

Keats thus "acculturates" the marvels that for Wordsworth had been almost entirely discoveries in a real, not conventionally metaphoric, natural world.

Wordsworth's literary originality consists principally not in his recording of new perceptions into nature but in his representing with acute self-awareness unique qualities of human responses to natural phenomena. Wordsworth opened himself to the charge of "egoism" because characteristically he did not present himself in his poetry as an "objective" observer. Quite to the contrary, he normally represents himself as bringing to his encounters with other people or natural phenomena very definite purposes, predilections, even prejudices—which means that his reader is not asked, cannot be asked, simply to identify with the poet-speaker. Probably the simplest illustration of this point is "We Are Seven," because it demonstrates Wordsworth's conscious willingness to represent himself as ridiculous in a fashion no poet before him had dared. But the less notorious and equally familiar "The Boy of Winander" is more revealing of the Wordsworthianism preference for discovery over invention.

These lines from *The Prelude* (but first published separately) change the poet's original representation of the experience as his own to that of another boy. This transposition blocks his readers from escaping into mere vicarious subjectivity. We can identify with "the boy" only at one remove. By "withdrawing" himself from what was in fact his own experience Wordsworth encourages his reader to recognize the special "bias" of the experiencer to be part of the experience reported. This is what makes the unexpectedness of the major occurrence so persuasive.

> when a lengthened pause
> Of silence came and baffled his best skill,
> Then sometimes, in that silence while he hung
> Listening, a gentle shock of mild surprise
> Has carried far into his heart the voice
> Of mountain torrents; or the visible scene
> Would enter unawares into his mind,
> With all its solemn imagery, its rocks,
> Its woods, and that uncertain heaven, received
> Into the bosom of the steady lake.[9]

The boy's intent purposefulness (to evoke the owls' responses) leaves him vulnerable, as it were, to the unsought entry into him of the "sounds of mountain torrents" and the imagery of the dusky scene. Because the poem has enabled us to perceive "objectively" both the experiencer and what he experiences (not just a subjective perspective), it dramatizes powerfully the reciprocality of encounter, showing how a human being may enter into nature and nature may enter into a human being.

"The Boy of Winander" illustrates the romantic focus upon human individuality as, paradoxically, likely to be obscured by subjectivity. Romantic individuality is an integrity of being best representable through engagement with what is other than itself, because it is individuality conceived as existing through interdependencies. From this view originate Wordsworth's characteristic poems of meetings with other human beings, such as the old Leech Gatherer and the Solitary Reaper, as well as the stories of the Idiot Boy, Peter Bell, the Brothers, and Michael. Each of these poems offers to the reader a vision of singular experiences that occurred because of a unique interrelation of individual character and particularized natural circumstances. The "significance" of such poetry lies in specific "discoveries," rather than in any affirmation of traditional forms of belief, conventionalized wisdom, or universal principles of philosophy or psychology. Wordsworth's best "nature" poems evoke "nothing more" than imaginings of how we may live discoveringly.

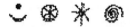

six

Malthusian Visions

Thomas Malthus, author of *An Essay on Population*, first published in 1798, was in several respects a quintessential romantic. His originality as a thinker arises from his claim that social analyses are valid only to the degree that they take account of the natural consequences of cultural activities. John Maynard Keynes situated Malthus in a major tradition of British "humane science" extending back to Locke and Hume and forward to Darwin. This tradition, Keynes observed, is distinguished "by a love of truth and a most noble lucidity, by prosaic sanity free from sentiment or metaphysic, and by an immense disinterestedness and public spirit."[1] This description may be overgenerous, especially in the light of Malthus's later career, in which he seems to have hewed closely to reactionary Tory ideologies and indulged his pessimism at the expense of the poor. Yet there is a "noble lucidity" in the first edition of *An Essay*, which focuses primarily on problems arising from the shift in the basis of European civilization from agriculture to industrial manufacturing.

Some of Malthus's methods deserve special notice. In the first place, he thinks in terms of populations. This is an approach with which we have become so familiar that we fail to recognize both its unusualness two hundred years ago and its potential political implications. Percy Bysshe Shel-

ley hated Malthusian doctrine as he understood it, but he, too, made use of "population thinking" in his most radical political poems. His *Mask of Anarchy* dramatically recommends passive resistance as a means of achieving political power, because, Shelley tells the working people of England, "Ye are many, they are few." The latter pronoun refers to England's rulers. Shelley was eager to condemn by name individuals in power, such as Lord Eldon and Castlereagh, as he does in this poem.

> I met Murder on the way—
> He had a mask like Castlereagh . . .
>
> Next came Fraud, and he had on,
> Like Eldon, an ermined gown . . .[2]

But Shelley never believed that individual politicians were primarily responsible for fundamental social evils. Nor did he believe such evils could be eliminated by individual "good" politicians. The condition of masses of people, large populations, was determined by themselves, not "great" leaders. This is probably why *The Mask of Anarchy* is the first poem to represent a vast number of ordinary people gathered together as something more significant than a "crowd" or a "mob" but as "the people" in a specific and cogent sense. Part of that significance derives from what Shelley perceives as the people's "earthliness," their closeness (to a degree, ironically, enforced upon them by their oppressors) to natural sources of strength and wisdom. Shelley represents the blood of the English shed at Peterloo as disfiguring the countenance of their mother, their land.

> As if their Own indignant Earth
> Which gave the sons of England birth
> Had felt their blood upon her brow,
> And shuddering with a mother's throe
>
> Had turned every drop of blood
> By which her face had been bedewed
> To an accent unwithstood,—
> As if her heart had cried aloud:

"Men of England, heirs of Glory,
Heroes of unwritten story,
Nurslings of one mighty Mother,
Hopes of her, and one another; . . ."[3]

Throughout *An Essay on Population* Malthus insists that not all the difficulties that human beings suffer derive from social institutions and bad rulers; some social problems are rooted in the conditions of the natural world. This view, however opposed to Shelleyan political ideals, accords with a fundamental romantic "ideology," that political attitudes must be grounded in awareness of every human society's peculiar interrelations with its natural environment.[4] The resulting sociopolitical recommendations of romantics may be as antithetical as Malthus's and Shelley's, but they are linked by an informed skepticism about merely political solutions to major social problems and an acute awareness of the physical circumstances in which social groups must function, as well as of the possible effects upon those circumstances of specific social actions.

Malthus, furthermore, invariably considers social issues *developmentally* in time. His fundamental argument, that population if unchecked increases more rapidly than means of subsistence, is presented as a historical truth. Malthus focuses on processes that operate over time, often long spans of time: he can speak casually of "only a single century." Present-day predictions that, for example, Bangladesh's current population of 114 million in an area the size of Wisconsin will in less than thirty years total 250 million would not startle Malthus. Indeed, by thinking developmentally and in terms of populations, he achieved his troubling but continuingly relevant position as a social commentator. Whether he is right or wrong about particular statistical facts matters very little in comparison to the value of his temporally oriented critiques focused on consequences for the physical environment of specific social practices.

Malthus's target in his 1798 *An Essay on the Principle of Population* was William Godwin. Godwin was at that time the principal English spokesman for progressive, perfectabilitarian, utopianist political ideals. He was England's leading intellectual "leftist." Had Malthus written fifty years later, his target might well have been a more important adulator of "progress," such as Karl Marx. Marx certainly hated Malthus, called him "the great destroyer of all hankerings after human development," misrep-

resented his arguments, and bequeathed to Marxists (until very recently indeed) a disastrously blind hostility to Malthusian hypotheses and observations. In all this, however, Marx was scarcely different from other liberal and progressive social thinkers. The more than two billion people on earth today (in Malthus's lifetime the total world population did not reach a billion) who live in conditions of starvation or malnutrition are to a considerable degree the beneficiaries of these anti-Malthusian idealists. Recent estimates are that the world's population is increasing at close to 2 percent per year (about 90 million people), while the production of such staple foods as cereals are increasing at under 1 percent a year; not surprisingly, in the past two decades at least 200 million people have starved to death. None of this proves that progressive and liberal ideas ought to be trashed, but it must compel honest people to examine the grounds on which Malthus challenges us to think through the possible consequences for nature of fundamental sociopolitical decisions.

Malthus's critique of Godwin is the first analysis of a utopian social plan that systematically tests its ideals against the realities of biological life. What Malthus says of Godwin is, mutatis mutandis, applicable to Plato's Republic, or Karl Marx's classless society—in fact, to virtually every utopian scheme. These idealizings disregard the natural effects in time that their successful implementation would produce. Malthus's test, however, is now frequently applied to practical proposals for social betterment. It is a rare town meeting these days in which an environmental impact study is not discussed. Nor is the collapse of Marxist regimes of Eastern Europe unconnected with problems Malthus posed. When people today demand to know the ecological effects of social or political projects, they are asking for Malthusian assessments.

Malthus's most telling argument against Godwin—which would be equally effective against the idealizations of Plato, Marx, or Reagan—occurs in the tenth chapter of the first edition of *An Essay*, in which he suggests that we may recognize "how little Mr. Godwin has turned the attention of his penetrating mind to the real state of man on earth" by suggesting that we imagine Godwin's "beautiful system" realized in "all its purity."[5]

Let us suppose all the causes of misery and vice in this island removed. War and contention cease. Unwholesome trades and manufactories do not exist. Crowds no longer collect together in great and pestilent cities for purposes of court intrigue, of commerce, and vicious gratifications. Simple, healthy, and rational amusements take the place of drinking, gaming, and debauchery. . . . Every house is clean, airy, sufficiently roomy, and in a healthy situation. All men are equal. The labours of luxury are at an end. And the necessary labours of agriculture are shared amicably among all. . . . the spirit of benevolence, guided by impartial justice, will divide this produce among all the members of the society according to their wants . . . sufficient to preserve them in health, strength, and spirits. (135)

Malthus then suggests that this utopia will have the added advantage of endorsing Godwin's belief that marriage is a fraud, so that "the commerce of the sexes" will be "established on the principles of the most perfect freedom." Malthus goes out of his way to make clear his agreement (unlike many of Godwin's conservative critics) with Godwin that such conditions would not lead to "promiscuous intercourse." He merely observes pleasantly that this happy society will be "favourable upon the whole to population." So we may assume that such a society would, as readily as most societies whose history we know, probably double in population every generation—say, every twenty-five years. The specific period of time is not essential—what matters is conceiving of the utopian situation historically, developmentally, in terms not merely of one generation but of that generation's offspring. Malthus urges us to continue imagining:

> Difficult, however, as it might be to double the average produce of the island in twenty-five years, let us suppose it effected. At the expiration of the first period, therefore, the food, though almost entirely vegetable, would be sufficient to support in health the doubled population of fourteen millions. . . . During the next period of doubling, where will the food be found to satisfy the importunate demands of the increasing numbers? Where is the fresh land to turn up? Where is the dressing necessary to improve that which is already in cultivation? (137)[6]

This is not so good, but "during the next period of doubling, where will the food be found to satisfy . . . the increasing number?" In a hundred years it will be 112 million who must find nourishment instead of 7 million. In this historical vision the "beautiful fabric of imagination vanishes at the severe touch of truth." Malthus then describes the foreseeable

reality, which, however unappealing to well-fed social philosophers, is not an inaccurate rendering of the conditions in much of our world today.

> The hateful passions that had vanished reappear. The mighty law of self-preservation expels all the softer and more exalted emotions of the soul. . . . The corn is plucked before it is ripe, or secreted in unfair proportions, and the whole black train of vices that belong to falsehood are immediately generated. Provisions no longer flow in for the support of the mothers with a large family. The children are sickly from insufficient food. (138)

Finally Malthus reiterates his fundamental point: the disaster is not caused by imperfect social institutions. "No monopoly had been created of those advantages which reason directs to be left in common. No man had been goaded to the breach of order by unjust laws." Yet, so powerful is the force of natural reality that within a few generations "violence, oppression, falsehood, misery, every hateful vice, and every form of distress, which degrade and sadden the present state of society, seems to have been generated by the most imperious circumstances . . . independent of all human regulation" (138).

Malthus has been so vilified and misrepresented that it is important to insist that he takes no pleasure in these dark visions of torment. Nor does he himself espouse all the reactionary politics that often have unjustly been blamed on him, especially by those unwilling to confront his basic arguments. Malthus is very much a man of his time in that he would like to see the condition of humankind improved. His objection to utopianist believers in "social progress" is that they perpetrate a vicious fraud. He believes that if they attain the power to do what they wish, the result will be the opposite of their promises: widespread poverty, hunger, despair, injustice, fear. The ruins of Eastern Europe and the Soviet Union are evidence of precisely the fraudulence that Malthus feared lurked in the heart of "progressive" ideologies.[7]

It may seem bizarre to turn from such polluted desolation to associate Malthus's relentless vision with Samuel Taylor Coleridge's story of quieting his weeping child by showing him the moon in "The Nightingale." Yet to understand the romantic poets we need to recognize the congruence of these two visions. Coleridge brings his child into his poem because he is concerned not merely with one instant in his own life, and not merely with *his* life. The quality of his child's life, moreover, is what matters most profoundly to him. Dorothy Wordsworth plays an analogous role for Wordsworth in "Tintern Abbey," which is concerned with more than the poet's private, personal experience, no matter how intense that may be. The poets perceive the individual and individual experience as fully meaningful only in terms of larger social and natural relationships. The ideological commitments of the romantic poets are founded in these attitudes, which put a premium on one's responsibility to family, friends, fellow citizens, and those who come after us.

This helps to explain the poets' attention to the interaffectivity of the political and the natural. To the romantic poets, ongoing natural processes matter very much to the quality of our lives, and so matter very much to every human being. Malthus's argument, in essence, is that human beings in their political arrangements ought to recognize their responsibilities in relation to the facts of natural reproduction and subsistence. Yet for him this does not exclude religious belief. In certain respects, the latter portions of *An Essay on Population* are among its most intriguing pages, though they are usually neglected even by the few literary critics who remember Malthus. What makes these pages interesting is, first, Malthus's sense that for all his marshaling of population statistics, ethical meaning must finally be grounded in individual acts, desires, choices. Malthus's discussions of virtue and vice assure that the question of individual responsibility is not ignored even in a world seen as operating according to rigorous naturalistic principles. Malthus accommodates his religious convictions to his perception of the material reality of nature through a kind of evolutionary conception. Malthus's somewhat heterodox views (he explicitly rejected the idea of damnation) help to illuminate the significance of Keats's evolutionary cosmology in *Hyperion*. That cosmology, as several commentators have noticed, is closely linked with his celebrated speculation in a letter about life as a vale of soul-making.

> Call the world if you Please "The vale of Soul-making" then you will find out the use of the world. . . . I say *"soul making"* Soul as distinguished from an Intelligence—There may be intelligences or sparks of the divinity in millions—but they are not Souls till they acquire identities, till each one is personally itself. . . . How then are Souls to be made? How then are these sparks which are God to have identity given them—so as ever to possess

a bliss peculiar to each ones individual existence? How, but by the medium of a world like this? . . . Do you now see how necessary a World of Pains and troubles is to school an Intelligence and make it a Soul? A Place where the heart must feel and suffer in a thousand diverse ways![8]

It is almost as if Keats had been reading Malthus. Malthus had asked, "Ought we not then to correct our crude and puerile ideas of Infinite Power from the contemplation of what we actually see existing?" What we see in nature, he points out, are processes of development. "Ought we not to conclude that to the Creator, almighty as he is, a certain process may be necessary, a certain time (or what appears to us as time) may be requisite . . . for his high purpose?" (18.201). Taking this perspective, Malthus says he is inclined to think of "the world and this life as the mighty process of God, not for the trial, but for the creation and formation of mind, a process necessary to awaken inert, chaotic matter into spirit" (202).

Malthus's and Keats's speculations resonate because both display a characteristic romantic sense for the interdependence of mind and body conceived in a developing relationship within a dynamic environment. For Malthus, body and mind "both seem to be forming and unfolding themselves at the same time," so that one may reasonably "suppose that God is constantly occupied in forming mind out of matter" (202). None of the later romantic poets share the firmness of Malthus's Christian outlook (or the harshness of his conservative views), but the conviction he expresses here is congruent with their thinking—for example, with the direction of the questioning articulated by Keats in his Hyperion poems. Malthus's ideas, in fact, may help to clarify the special intricacy of these unfinished works. Because Keats, like the other romantic poets, does not dissociate political and cultural judgments from judgments on humankind's relation to the natural environment, his poems necessarily address the ways in which developments of mind and matter function interdependently.

Thanks to Hermione de Almeida's recent book *Romantic Medicine and John Keats*,[9] which traces in meticulous detail the fashion in which "the evolution of organic life is a persistent subject and nascent metaphor for poetic creativity" throughout Keats's short career, it is possible briefly to refer to the importance of romantic evolutionary thought. The cosmological basis, of course, had been laid by Kant in 1755 when he proposed that the solar system as it presently exists is the result of a condensing nebula. Forty years later the French astronomer Laplace gave the "nebular hypothesis" a mathematical and physical basis. Soon afterward William Herschel, the English astronomer whose work was well known to the romantic poets, proposed that the stars as well as the solar system resulted from nebular contraction. Meanwhile botanical and zoological research was bringing to the fore evolutionary concepts of life on earth. The pervasive influence of evolutionary thought in the romantic era has been underestimated because of its Lamarckian bias. That Darwinian evolution has proven to be scientifically more productive, however, should not be allowed to obscure the strongly developmental cast of romantic thinking about the processes of life in time. That cast, for example, distinguishes the "environmental historicism" of the romantics from that of their neoclassic forerunners.[10]

Romantic Lamarckian evolution identified life and activity. The impetus for evolution came from within an organism, which changed as an individual (though passing on its developments by heredity), through a need of that individual creature to meet environmental demands. Basic to this view was a conception of the natural world as extraordinarily changeable, in a continual process of composition and decomposition. In this perspective the interactivity of living beings is conceived of as profoundly penetrative and absorptive. Relationships are regularly perceived as, to use Keats's word, *interassimilative*.[11]

Romantic poetry favors interassimilative structures and imagery, striving to be responsive in its verbal dissolutions and reconstitutings to the continuity of change, which, for the romantic poets, is the essential characteristic of phenomenal reality. In Coleridge's celebrated words, the imagination "dissolves, diffuses, dissipates, in order to recreate." Obviously evolutionary conceptions are appropriate, even necessary, to the cosmologies undergirding such views. This is why the poets so insist upon the need for a psychological adaptivity or receptivity—in Keats's compelling phrase, *negative capability*.

Romantic poetry must overflow limited boundaries, be shaped around continuously self-transformative structures, because only thus can it adequately represent and embody the fittedness of humankind to "nature" conceived as perpetually decomposing and recomposing itself.

Wordsworth and Shelley in their poetry use literally hundreds of metrical structures and variations upon them. They are poets not of disorder but of superabundant forms. The wondrous organization of "nature" (which the poets' formal superabundance echoes) in the romantic view is not fixed and static but continuous, multiform processes of interchange and self-transformation. "History" for the romantics, therefore, is not only applicable to human events—it is as significant for natural events. The romantic objection to purely rationalistic explanations was their tendency to mystify the continuous transformativeness of being, whether in the natural world or in human consciousness. Acts of imagination arising from an adaptive receptivity, on the contrary, enhance what Wordsworth called "the sentiment of being," the satisfying feeling of continuity of change within a self tempered by and attuned to the vital continuity of an ever–self-transfiguring environment.

There is nothing soft or sentimental in this conception. It acknowledges that dissolution entails death. It does not evade the ferocities of natural existence. As Keats wrote to J. H. Hamilton,

> I saw
> Too far into the sea, where every maw
> The greater on the less feeds evermore.—
> But I saw too distinct into the core
> Of an eternal fierce destruction. . . .
>
> Still do I that most fierce destruction see,
> —The shark at savage prey,—the hawk at pounce,—
> The gentle robin, like a pard or ounce,
> Ravening a worm, . . .[12]

Even more powerful are the pain and loss intrinsic to evolutionary processes evoked in the *Hyperion* poems. For the romantics, nevertheless, the junction of the continuity of conscious mind's mutability with the continuity of our natural environment's mutability produces the most inspiring and valuable human creations. In the *Hyperion* poems as emphatically as in Wordsworth's "Home at Grasmere" the power of human imagination is shown as derived from a consciousness of belonging to—not defining itself by its transcendence of—its physical environment. The younger Wordsworth and Keats are equally convinced that the principal responsibility borne by poets is to help us enjoy to the full the world, which, however much a vale of soul-making through pain and suffering, is our appropriate dwelling place, where we find our happiness or not at all.

This does not mean that self-conscious "mind" and external "nature" are indistinguishable. One cannot speak of things fitting unless they are distinct. Coleridge's famous phrase about "the one life within us and abroad" is in fact his rather characteristic oversimplification of a more complex and fundamental romantic view. Unlike the other romantics, Coleridge's principal enterprise was to fuse humanity and the world in a transcendent Christianity. This is not only why he accused Wordsworth of "pantheism" but also why in his criticism, notably in the *Biographia Literaria*, he so frequently misunderstood and misrepresented his friend's poetic purposes and achievements. Equally revealing is the relative triviality of his few remarks on the poetry of the younger romantics. Lamb, Hunt, Hazlitt, and even journalistic reviewers like Jeffrey made many acute and valuable (if not always sympathetic) comments on poems by Byron, Shelley, and Keats. That Coleridge, esteemed as the finest of romantic critics, has so little to say about his younger contemporaries' poetry that is not either conventional or off the mark is a circumstance that calls for careful analysis.

How poor a guide Coleridge is to his leading contemporary poets is suggested by his difficulty in dealing with what is their highest aspiration—to be capable of intense ambivalences. I have suggested that one basis for this ideal is revealed by Malthus's critique of his age's celebration of sociopolitical progress as a terrifying oversimplification. Both natural life and human life are enormously complicated phenomena. Commitment to simplified ideas of "progress" is in fact an abdication of humankind's complex and multivalent responsibilities. It is the ambivalences inherent in these intricate responsibilities (beginning in the duality of humans as both natural and cultural creatures) that the younger romantic poets explore intensely in their final poems. Keats, perhaps because of his training as a physician, and almost certainly because of the disease with which he was stricken, focused his explorations on physical pain.

He never surrendered his early commitment to the belief in poetry as a means of soothing and healing. But from the beginning he recognized

that poetry could function to heal and soothe, could be a friend to humanity, only because there were injuries, agitations, hostilities, sicknesses, and losses to be soothed and healed. His intensifying literariness in the course of his brief career as a poet seems to accompany a growing imaginative responsiveness to the medical wisdom to which he had been exposed—that, in his stark phrase, "women have cancers." One might also regard the continuing thrust of Keats's poetry as a development of the Wordsworthian effort to humanize the natural world—not in the false manner of imposing on it cultural artifices but by articulating a fittingness between natural-physical and cultural-psychic energies. Keats tries to naturalize the humanizing imagination, to reveal the naturalness of imagining made possible by culture. But to appreciate fully Keats's advancing of this Wordsworthian ethos, we must consider his particular accomplishments in relation to the parallel endeavors of Byron and Shelley.

Appendix: Attacks on Malthus

The principal cause of vilifications of Malthus was indubitably the use or misuse of his ideas by those with "reactionary" political commitments and often by morally repulsive people. Some of Malthus's own later writings, like those of Wordsworth, furthermore, did much to justify the savagery of attacks on him by "liberal" thinkers (which would include social commentators as "conservative" as Cobbett). Malthus's plan proposed in his 1803 vast expansion of the 1798 *Essay* for the gradual abolition of the poor laws, for instance, may rightly be condemned as inhumane in itself and as encouraging tendencies of selfish and socially repressive politicians and social theorists.

The 1803 edition also introduced the subtler and more complicated issue of birth control, with Malthus suggesting, as he had done nowhere in the 1798 version, that because "moral restraint" was the only "virtuous mode" of escaping the evil results of population, it is "our obligation to practise it." This was, of course, to admit the possibility of conscious human control of a process that he had previously described as if it were a biological necessity beyond deliberate human management—"laws inherent in the nature of man, and absolutely independent of all human regulation."

Malthus, I believe, may with some fairness be faulted for not developing this point more cogently. But equal fairness would require us to recognize that during his lifetime he was almost never condemned by his many detractors for failing to emphasize the value of contraception and birth control practices. After all, in Malthus's day one could be imprisoned for publicly advocating birth control—the first birth control clinic in the United States, we ought to remember, was opened only in 1916. Yet in the final chapter of the 1798 *Essay* (as at other points in his writings) one perceives Malthus's awareness of the personal, individual meaning of "population pressures": in chapter 19 he hypothesizes with extraordinary prescience our century's biological discovery that not even two grains of wheat, let alone two human beings, are identical. I, at any rate, often feel a tension between Malthus's sympathetic disposition, which appears even in the condemnations of Godwin's ideas in passages I have quoted earlier, and the rigorous consequences of his rational conclusions, as when in the nineteenth chapter, for instance, he speaks of the value of being alive to "the wants and wishes" of his fellow beings and insists that "kind and amiable affections . . . dignify the human character even more than the possession of the highest talents." It remains true, nonetheless, that Malthus rather characteristically interpreted American population statistics, which had been cited in support of democratic institutions, so as to draw a frightening picture of China-like overpopulation in the New World. And, in stark contrast to Shelley's confidence in the people I have illustrated with his *Mask of Anarchy*, Malthus was not above fearmongering by creating the impression that "revolutionary" ideals inevitably entailed voraciously destructive mobs.

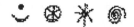

seven

Refiguring Reason

In now directing my perhaps weary reader's attention to poetry of the younger romantic poets, Byron, Shelley, and Keats, I shall not be proposing daring new readings of several famous poems. I hope, rather, to suggest how attitudes fostered by ecological criticism enable us to respond with renewed enthusiasm not merely to this poetry but also to critical commentaries on it. No professional critic rereads familiar poems with anything even faintly resembling innocence. Not only do we know each poem well (sometimes even by heart) but how we understand its words is decisively determined by a multitude of critiques we have read—sometimes, I suspect, comments with which we disagreed having influenced us more than those closer to our own ideas. An older critic like myself also reads poetic texts through a dense screen of his previous analyses. The soporific result of entrapment in one's own critical past is all too familiar to bored undergraduates.

A major purpose of literary criticism, we tend to forget, is to overcome the deadening effect of repeated critical analyses by turning those experiences into a means of reacquiring a freshness of response matching the unfading vitality of fine poetry. If we can find means for innovatively reconsidering how we have already engaged with a poem, we may successfully challenge the false innocence of our young students. For they are really only ignorant, which means they respond according to simplified patterns of internalized prejudice, of whose structuring of their thinking and feeling they are unaware. Ecological criticism is peculiarly valuable for facilitating such reconsiderations. It is open-ended, its definite readings never pretending to be definitive. It is essentially inclusive, even historically, because it is developmental—that is, it employs the process of its own evolution out of earlier understandings. These qualities enable ecological criticism to be proactive as well as reactive, emphasizing what might be called a fine poem's epigenetic character, its capacity to "grow" and change through the process of being critically examined.[1]

The principal theme I now seek to develop is how and to what effect the younger romantic poets developmentally revised the proto-ecological innovations of Wordsworth and Coleridge that I have already outlined. A striking difference between the two generations is the blatant literariness of the younger poets. Coleridge and Wordsworth introduced new kinds of lyricism, new kinds of narrative poetry, and in a variety of ways began redefining what had been regarded as traditional functions of poetry.[2] The almost defiant literariness of the last, most ambitious poems composed by Byron, Shelley, and Keats seems to originate in the later poets' testing of the significance of these innovations, an extension and development of their predecessors' practices through more probing questioning of how the highest cultural aspirations may connect to the most fundamental processes of natural being. These developmental revisions were, of course, encouraged and given an edge of ideological ferocity by the younger poets' conviction that Wordsworth and Coleridge had betrayed the sociopolitical commitments that had accompanied their aesthetic adventurousness, and which in the reactionary post-Waterloo era needed to be asserted against the pressure of seemingly ever more successful political oppressions.

Percy Shelley's "Triumph of Life," ironically broken off by the poet's drowning, and John Keats's "Fall of Hyperion," the unfinished attempt shortly before his death to recast his uncompleted "Hyperion," both employ the medieval form of dream vision. Both romantic visions are indebted to Dante's *Divine Comedy*, but both are entirely secularized. These are literary dreams of unmystical poets without belief in a transcendent deity. Unlike Dante's, these dreams cannot authenticate or validate; Shelley and Keats understand—and expect readers to understand—that their visions are "nothing more" than naturalistic dreams.

Both poems, then, may be called "archaistic," if by the term one means deliberate resurrection of a recognizedly obsolete artistic form. In reanimating a discarded mode, the younger romantics dramatize the dubiety of any authoritative support for their imaginings. These accounts of dreams within dreams do not require from a reader any suspension of disbelief. Unlike "The Rime of the Ancient Mariner," these narratives present themselves not as fictions but as reports of visions as natural phenomena, in somewhat the same sense that hallucinations are "natural." The visions propose the possibility of a surprising enlightenment through imaginings recursively coherent although not conventionally "reasonable."

Because they recognize no transcendent divinity, the romantics in their dream visions offer only a perspective, an alternative way of specifying and assessing reality. Because the poems admit no intellectual basis but the poets' imaginations, their dreams make no claim to universality, their value depending on whether they sharpen their readers' skill at determining humankind's ever-shifting activities in an undivine natural world. So in concluding his introduction to "The Fall of Hyperion" Keats recognizes that his audience will decide whether his dream functions as hallucination or precious intuition.

> Whether the dream now purposed to rehearse
> Be Poet's or Fanatic's will be known
> When this warm scribe my hand is in the grave.[3]

To be evaluated in "The Fall of Hyperion" is an account of a dream of dreaming of a dream. This regressive, self-enclosed envisioning, the antithesis of any rationalized analysis, is necessary because the poet refuses to accept any unassailable transcendent or metahistorical position from which to describe natural phenomena or philosophic explanations of them. Visionary experience may offer insight into both, but the experience may be mere evidence of derangement. Keats's very reports of his difficulty in reporting increase our difficulty in judging the value of his judgments.

> Without stay or prop,
> But my own weak mortality, I bore
> The load of this eternal quietude,
> The unchanging gloom and three fixed shapes

Ponderous upon my senses a whole moon.
. . . .
Oftentimes I prayed
Intense, that death would take me from the vale
And all its burthens. Gasping with despair
Of change, hour after hour I cursed myself—
(2.388–99)

Throughout these painful dream-vision fragments, then, we are encouraged not passively to accept conclusions but to undertake the burdens of constructing our own recognizedly provisional assessments of the poet's mode of assessing. The poem's self-consciousness invites us into onerous engagements with questionable representations of the functions of self-consciousness.

Odd as this procedure may at first appear, it makes sense when we recognize that Keats and Shelley are not trying to escape from reasoned discourse but to evaluate its uses *naturalistically*. These poets dream to evaluate reason and reason's products, striving to determine what it has achieved and what it has not, what it can achieve and what it cannot. This may put them at odds with some contemporary critics, but it does not put them at odds with contemporary scientists who pursue their disciplined study of natural phenomena by trying to challenge the preconceptions built into their own systematized rationality. It is the seekers' self-skeptical slant of mind (implying a basic confidence in their aspirations), rather than any particular knowledge, or intuitive insight, that aligns romantic speculations with some of the preoccupations of present-day scientists. Like these scientists, the romantic poets are less concerned than modern critics with the self-delusive qualities of language and with philosophizing about covert ideological biases. Their primary aim is to comprehend how we understand the nature of the physical world—out of which all cultures, all languages, and all ideologies are constructed.

To measure the value of our reasoning efforts to attain such comprehension—to judge, that is, how most effectively to exercise (on ourselves and on our environment) the systematic efficacies of self-consciousness—the romantics tried to get outside of the reasoning process itself. Religious belief offers one such means. The English romantics, however, were not religious believers. It was only by imagining, or envisioning, or dreaming

that they could assess "from outside" the rational workings of human consciousness in a universe they conceived of as purely natural, without divine sanction or transcendent order. Or, to describe their specific purposes more concretely, they sought poetic forms that might lure their readers into evaluating their understanding of how we usefully or injuriously apply our reason to the physical nature of things. The recursively embedded dreams constituting "The Fall of Hyperion" and "The Triumph of Life" that seek to illuminate how we reason about nature do not offer practical "solutions" to society's pressing problems of hunger, disease, injustice, and brutalization. Yet because the poems try to evaluate the rational systems that underlie social practices, they neither evade nor disguise the relevance of such practical problems to their purposes. Both poems, therefore, address the question of what may be the appropriate social functions of poetry, defining their articulations against the shortcomings of others' imaginative discourse. Keats's narrator explicitly condemns "mock lyricists, large self-worshippers / And careless hectorers in proud bad verse" (1.207–8). Shelley dramatizes the failures of Jean-Jacques Rousseau by representing him as a decayed tree stump.

Both "The Fall of Hyperion" and "The Triumph of Life," besides being inconclusive because unfinished, are in themselves imagistically ambivalent, offering pictures of astonishing grandeur and beauty intermingled with representations of seemingly inescapable fear, paralysis, horror, and despair.[4] The antithetical conditions, moreover, are presented as intrinsic to life processes. In Keats's view, these processes are evolutionary in character. His poem tells of "divinities" who, "by the law of nature" lose their potency as their places are usurped by other manifestations of energy. We read of the overthrow of the Titans by the Olympian gods, significantly, from the perspective of those abruptly and incomprehensibly disempowered. Since the Olympian deities have by Keats's time themselves long been superseded, we are directed toward recognizing the Olympians' "fresh perfection," their superiority to their Titanic predecessors, as foreshadowing their own future downfall. The natural inevitability of their disempowerment almost exactly parallels that which Mahmud in Shelley's *Hellas* comes to perceive for himself when he understands that the ultimate destruction of Turkish strength was implicit in its triumph centuries before.

The "Hyperion" poems, however, focus on "divinities," not historical figures. The nature of such divinities, though, has bothered more than one critic, since, as I have already observed, nobody had believed in them for a very long time, and their divine powers are subject to natural law. Of Hyperion, for instance, we are told in the first poem

> Fain would he have commanded, fain took throne
> And bid the day begin, if but for change.
> He might not:—No, though a primeval God:
> The sacred seasons might not be disturb'd.
>
> (1.290–93)

Despite such uncertainties, few readers or critics seem to have regarded the Titans and Olympians as allegorical: Keats somehow succeeds in allowing us to take these forgotten gods "literally," as what they purport to be, not as "standing for" something else. I would suggest that Keats accomplishes this remarkable feat by creating a kind of an adult analogue of what the psychologist D. W. Winnicott has called a "potential space," the overlapping for a very young child of fantasy and reality, a conjunction that facilitates the child's discovery of what is outside because it sustains the child's sense of omnipotence, of creating what it finds. This confident relationship to the external world, rather than passive compliance with a purely exterior reality, allows the child happily to find a niche for itself in what exists beyond it.[5] I suggest the analogy because Keats's success in luring his readers into accepting as nonallegorical his vanished divinities is dependent upon their representation *as* figures imagined or envisioned, yet not for that reason irrelevant to external, material reality. All the intense sorrow, suffering, and pain in the poems is undergone, moreover, by figures whose impressively humanlike beauty is emphasized whether they are victorious or defeated.

The story of the Olympians' success as Keats tells it is less a story of conflict than the arbitrary and upsetting appearance of a heretofore unrealized beauty—perfection of being—superseding other perfectly majestic and beautiful beings. This process of triumph (that seems to doom beautiful conquerors in their turn to unpredictable replacement) is for most of us the worst horror of evolution: marvelous forms are produced only to become victims of other marvelous forms. Why this is so terrible is revealed in the lament of Keats's young Titaness Clymene. She evokes less the misery of defeat than a more intense pain: awareness of the "justice" of being unexpectedly superseded. Her anguished experience of recog-

nizing a beauty beyond her capacities focuses the terrible ambiguity intrinsic to evolutionary "progress" for self-conscious creatures. She tells how she sat down on the seashore

> and took a mouthed shell
> And murmur'd into it, and made melody—
> O melody no more! for while I sang,
> And with poor skill let pass into the breeze
> The dull shell's echo, from a bowery strand
> Just opposite, an island of the sea,
> There came enchantment with the shifting wind,
> That did both drown and keep alive my ears.
> I threw my shell away upon the sand,
> And a wave fill'd it, as my sense was fill'd
> With that new blissful golden melody.
> A living death was in each gush of sounds . . .
>
> (2.270–81)

Keats represents this "progress" of living deaths of successive perfections (as must anyone with a purely naturalistic understanding of the cosmos) as in itself meaningless. The sequence of supersessions leads to no end, has no justification beyond the mere fact of its occurrence. This (more than the relatively superficial horror of massive destruction of natural creatures in the struggle for existence) is the blackest terror at the heart of evolutionary thought. It is a terror, Keats recognized, that can be fully experienced only by those capable of passionately admiring the beauty and wonder that natural evolution produces—purposelessly to be obliterated.

The continuing interest of the seemingly belletristic "Hyperion" poems resides in their unflinching focus upon events evolutionary in character. In "The Fall of Hyperion," Keats's poignant personalizing of evolution seen from the perspective of a "victim" never shrinks into representation of mere private experience, mere personal trauma. More wonderfully, the poem uses self-doubt and personal pain as a means to imaginative recognition of global or cosmic principles baffling in their paradoxicality. As we know from the "Epistle to Reynolds," Keats perceived all too clearly the brutality inherent in the struggle for survival, a ferocity vividly dramatized by Schopenhauer when he wrestled with the meaning of evolution.

In Java he saw an immense field entirely covered with skeletons, and took it to be a battle-field. However, they were nothing but skeletons of large turtles five feet long, three feet broad, and of equal height. These turtles come this way from the sea, in order to lay their eggs, and are then seized by wild dogs. . . . with their united strength, these dogs lay them on their backs, tear open their lower armour. . . and devour them alive. But then a tiger often pounces on the dogs. Now all this misery is repeated thousands and thousands of times, year in and year out. For this, then, are these turtles born. What is the point of this whole scene of horror?[6]

Awful as this scene is, it lacks the experiential self-consciousness of anguish evoked by Keats's apparently gentler representation of Clymene's sorrowful joy. The intensity and significance of that ambivalence is deepened by the depiction of Moneta in "The Fall of Hyperion," when she displays her

> wan face
> Not pined with human sorrows, but bright-blanched
> By an immortal sickness which kills not;
> It works a constant change, which happy death
> Can put no end to; deathwards progressing
> To no death.
>
> (2.257–61)[7]

Keats's Moneta is a version of Mnemosyne, traditionally identified as the mother of the muses. Moneta, however, displays principally the wonderful/terrible capacity to keep alive through memory the supersession of her race. If we have no faith beyond naturalism, we will be unable to perceive any purpose in the endlessly destructive "advance" she articulates, deathward progressing to no death, a goal far more troubling than the mere quiescence of Freud's Thanatos. As the poem's own beauty demonstrates, however, the absence of purpose need not obscure our dazzled pleasure at the marvels it produces or the wondrousness of its ways of transforming itself—if we have the courage to live in joy and sorrow at once.

"The Fall of Hyperion" in this respect at least is profoundly illuminating of the romantic willingness to reject as humanly incomplete both the

temptations of faith in transcendent deity and of nihilistic pessimism that ends in nothing beyond a teeth-gritting existential stoicism. Both in effect deny the agonizing complexity of a genuinely naturalistic vision, attainable in Keats's view only through imagination. Only imagination sustains ambivalent emotions arising from keen responsiveness to both the enchanting beauty and the implacable self-destructiveness of natural processes in which humans inescapably participate. This is why Keats's poet-dreamer "venoms all his days" by surrendering the deceptive relief of seeking "the pain alone, the joy alone, distinct."

Probably because it was broken off by Shelley's accidental violent death, "The Triumph of Life" displays its equivalent ambivalence more vividly in its details than in what remains of its structure. The song of sunrise that opens Shelley's poem, for example, depicts as stingingly as Clymene's story the birth of a beauty more terrible than Yeats conceived.[8] The pain in the beauty of Shelley's sunrise song, however, arises from exactly the opposite cause of that which wracks Keats's Titans. The sunrise is terrible because its unique "birth" is a repetition of an endless, meaningless "diurnal round."

> Swift as a spirit hastening to his task
>   Of glory and of good, the Sun sprang forth
> Rejoicing in his splendour, and the mask
>
> Of darkness fell from the awakened Earth.
> The smokeless altars of the mountain snows
>   Flamed above crimson clouds, and at the birth
>
> Of light, the Ocean's orison arose
>   To which the birds tempered their matin lay.
> . . . .
>   Isle, Ocean, and all things that in them wear
> The form and character of mortal mould
>   Rise as the Sun their father rose, to bear
>
> Their portion of the toil which he of old
>   Took as his own and then imposed on them; . . .[9]

For Shelley, repetitive cycles of natural processes threaten to undermine our joy in natural beauty. For him, the more we learn about nature, the more its reiterative meaninglessness will appall us. Ultimate horror lies not in the heart of darkness but in the heart of enlightened understanding of nature. The disturbing strength of Shelley's final poem arises from its pursuing beyond the merely personal Wordsworth's insight in "A Slumber Did My Spirit Seal." The romantics celebrate natural phenomena without shrinking from the terrible implications of materialistic naturalism. Lovingly they display the pleasures to be gained from the loveliest singularities of natural phenomena, that they know—and show—simultaneously embody destructively mechanistic processes.

The primary target of the cultural critique of "The Triumph" is the Enlightenment, the pan-European intellectual-political movement that Shelley cherished as the source of both his utopian social idealisms and his intellectual daring. He uses the Enlightenment-despised medieval dream vision as a means to represent himself as, for both good and ill, an inheritor of the Enlightenment ethos within an anti-Enlightenment poem. For the primary subject of "The Triumph of Life" is self-delusion. Specifically, Shelley delineates the cultural fostering of delusion that produces moral self-betrayals by impassioned idealists, such as he knew himself to be.

People who are most enlightened (as Paul de Man inadvertently reveals through his reading of "The Triumph") are likely to be most self-blinded. Breaking free of superstitiousness and the rigidities of feudal politics, Enlightenment thinkers based their ideological idealisms on what they took to be "the nature of things." Cultural arrangements of any ideological persuasion founded on what is "natural," however, chain themselves to a destructive "car of life," Shelley's brilliant image of the cultural empowerment of naturalism. His central exemplars are "enlightened despots" of the eighteenth century and their heirs, such as Napoleon, along with rationalistic and scientific social philosophers like Voltaire. All these are unconscious self-betrayers whose disciples are double dupes, because they misunderstand natural processes to be inherently progressive and beneficent. They are, in fact, characterized by purposeless indifference to human valuations.

There is, however, no easy alternative. There is no metanature, divine or otherwise. We are natural creatures. The consequences of our natural-

ness, however, are not what deists and utopian ideologues claimed. This is why Rousseau appears in "The Triumph of Life" as a degraded and self-mystified parody of Virgil in the *Divine Comedy*. Rousseau is that most ambiguous thing, a noble failure, an idealist overcome by his own heart, self-treasonous. He is a peculiarly dangerous self-victimizer because he is so tempting a model for others. Stricken by what he wrongly regards as his distinction from competing thinkers, who believed in their superiority to nature, he ends, no better than they, because he, too, misconceived his human nature.

Resurfacing here is a subtilized version of the admonition of "Lines Left upon a Seat": simultaneously suspect and revere yourself. Shelley's vision is both more complexly dramatic and more historically resonant than Wordsworth's. In "The Triumph," no anonymous melancholic but Europe's most celebrated advocate of "natural man" appears naturally deteriorated, able only to scorn with partial understanding other great philosophers and political rulers enslaved by the forces they feigned controlling because they were unable to master "the mutiny within." This puzzling phrase illuminates an essential innovation in the romantic conception of nature. For the romantics, "human nature" is, like external nature, dynamic, a process of transformation, a self-unfolding, a perpetual exfoliating. Every individual is fully human to the degree that he or she actively realizes and extends to its fullest his or her capacity for singular development.

If the essential reality of human nature is such evolving singularity, our internal existence will surely include "mutiny." The mutineers, however, will not be individualizing impulses. They will be, instead, the masked anarchs of "instinct" and internalized pressures to yield uniqueness to socialized conformities, commonly justified as "natural." These disguised opponents of humankind's authentic impulses inhibit individual transformational development. The alliance of the apparently opposite instinctual and social "conservatisms" lies in their common resistance to what uniqueness supremely manifests: change. Both "conservatisms" enforce the repetitive, cyclical aspects of nature that would confine the individual within an "orderliness" that is requisite to the continuities making up social and natural persistence. This limited order, however, is a self-entrapping reiteration of life leading to death, producing more life, leading to more death—ad infinitum. In such a system, as I once heard

Northrop Frye observe, life is nothing more than death's way of producing more dead bodies.

What if, however, one conceives of nature as something more than separated lives seeking death, something more than Eros's duplicitously cir-
cular return to the inactivity of Thanatos? What if one conceives of life as
diverse processes striving to sustain what we call ecosystems, complexes of
interactivity that enhance the power and endurance of their vitality
through a cooperative interplay of self-transforming individualities?
Then a hopeful prospect of successfully coordinating individuality and
social or material regularity emerges. The true "orderliness" of nature
then appears to be not the deadly mechanicalness of limited regularities
but the ever-surprising contingent interactions of differing and varying
vital rhythms. These unexpected patternings to "enlightened" rationaliz-
ers appear to be disruptive accidents, signs of disorganization. They are,
to the contrary, manifestations of a profounder organization, the intersecting of diverse, even opposed regularities. Within an ecosystem particular contingencies, including particular deaths, sustain more complex
and extensive vitalities. The radicalness of Shelley's vision is its perception
of nature as an ever-evanescent interplay of singularized entities constituted by the intermeshing of incommensurate systems. Nature so conceived is self-sustaining *because* it is continually self-transfiguring. Nature
so conceived is therefore hospitable to—because it is capable of being fostered by—the flourishing of human self-consciousness, justifying Paul
Valery's wonderful summation of this romantic reversal of Descartes:
"L'Homme pense; donc je suis," dit l'Univers.

One way of understanding Shelley's view is to regard it as analogous to
modern chaos theory, which deals with natural phenomena that are
unstable at every point (leaves fluttering to the ground, for example),
forms of order masquerading as randomness. The kind of order discovered beneath the appearance of randomness, however, will not be patterns
definable by linear equations. Such order, like that of turbulent phenomena, requires more complicated descriptive modes, which will seem
chaotic to those dependent on traditional logic and mechanistic cosmologies. Shelley's concern with the duplicities of anarchistic appearances carried him far beyond the simplicities of *concordia discors*, but he
of course knew nothing of chaos theory or of nonlinear equations or of
systems of scientific description constructed to accommodate changes in

rules of description in the act of describing. He had never heard of "sensitive dependence on initial conditions," which explains how gigantic effects result from tiny causes. The most enlightened science of Shelley's day was still basically mechanistic. It seemed, therefore, to reveal at the heart of nature only endless cycles of rigidly repetitive events. So Shelley was impelled to "poetic" vision, which was for him, in essence, the power of the human imagination to reconfigure its own structures of rational comprehension, what a neuroscientist like Gerald Edelman calls "bootstrapping." This self-reconfiguring carries the mind beyond the limits of the intellectual system from which it starts.

As P.M.S. Dawson has cogently argued, Shelley in "The Triumph" demonstrates that we need not be victims of the obvious cyclic processes that seem to dominate the physical cosmos.[10] We victimize ourselves when, like Rousseau, we mistakenly assume, for example, that the diurnal and seasonal cycles are the only cycles and are therefore absolute. Ecologists, however, recognize that "time" is far more complex than this. They perceive, simply, that the traditional four seasons are a crude approximation—more than four "seasons" are distinguishable on most parts of the earth, some of which have "more" seasons than others, and these, of course, vary from place to place on the globe. What we may here call "ecological time," however, is even more complicated than this, because the temporal ordering of any ecosystem is necessarily constituted by a variety of intersecting rhythms and tempos.

The major cycles of day and season, moreover, are "our" inventions and need not be thought of as absolute determinants. Dawson points out that "The Triumph of Life" insists dramatically through the image of the cone of night that what we perceive as the "diurnal round" is a creation of the earth itself. The illuminating irony of Rousseau's image of the traveler who hopes to find Venus appearing as the evening star on the same day the planet has appeared as the morning star is that such doubling would depend on conceiving the spinning of the earth and the rotation of the planets around the sun within a more encompassing ordering of cosmic relations than that from which derive the traditional names of "morning" and "evening" star.[11] The seemingly esoteric point exemplifies Shelley's awareness that a complete understanding of natural phenomena is likely to require something more than accurate knowledge of "the thing in itself," but, rather, accurate knowledge of the way in which each thing

107

participates in shifting sets of relations with other things. Imagination, for Shelley, is the psychic power enabling us to attain this kind of understanding, which requires a revision, or a series of revisions, in simplified conceptions of the regularity of nature's workings.

How one makes recognition of repetition function liberatively is illustrated near the beginning of "The Triumph of Life" when the narrator records his awareness of a repetitiveness in his private sensations. Through the consciousness that his very resistance to the earth's cyclic rotation is itself repetition, part of another cycle, the speaker opens himself to a new "vision":

> a strange trance over my fancy grew,
> Which was not slumber, for the shade it spread
>
> Was so transparent that the scene came through
> As clear as when a veil of light is drawn
> O'er evening hills they glimmer; and I knew
>
> That I had felt the freshness of that dawn,
> Bathed in the same cold dew my brow and hair
> And sate as thus upon that slope of lawn
>
> Under the self-same bough, and heard as there
> The birds, the fountains and the Ocean hold
> Sweet talk in music through the enamoured air.
> And then a Vision on my brain was rolled.
>
> (456.29–40)

Critics have not observed that the feeling of déja vu here enhances Wordsworthian superimpositions such as we are offered by "Tintern Abbey." There, the reiterated view contains for the poet "life and food for future years." Here in "The Triumph of Life" Shelley suggests how awareness of repetition offers to any of us freedom from imprisonment within the mechanical repetitiveness of natural processes, such as the diurnal round. The younger poet thus more explicitly represents imaginative self-consciousness as a nontranscendental act of liberation. The most powerful implication in this view, which Rousseau in Shelley's poem

is unable to grasp, is that imagination is above all else the power to refigure the very imaginative figurations through which we articulate explanations of the material systems making possible the existence of our consciousness.[12]

This capability for Shelley is neither a divine gift nor a peculiar talent solely of gifted individuals but a potential in any human being—a capability, however, easily blocked by internalized preconceptions. This at any rate is how I interpret the striking description of the dusty path along which a "great stream of people" hurry blind and deaf to the relief and refreshment offered by the lush natural landscape through which the road arbitrarily cuts. Shelley's vision thus opens with the very opposite of a Dantean dark wood. For the romantic, satisfying natural comfort is always accessible, ready at hand. The suffering travelers are self-deluded, self-victimized by their disregard of pleasures freely offered by nature:

> weary with vain toil and faint from thirst
> Heard not the fountains whose melodious dew
>
> Out of their mossy cells forever burst
> Nor felt the breeze which from the forest told
> Of grassy paths, and wood lawns interspersed
>
> With overarching elms and caverns cold,
> And violet banks where sweet dreams brood . . .
>
> (66–72)

The liberating imagination that Shelley would celebrate, then, derives from "nothing more than what we are" and is simply the complete exercise of our natural capacities as self-conscious beings. New visions are accessible because the imagination constituting them originates in awareness of arbitrary limitations imposed by conditions that give rise to it. This explains why in the introductory lines of "The Triumph of Life" it is not enough that the poet physically set himself against the rotation of the earth; the possibility of new vision depends also on his awareness of repeating his private opposition to the diurnal round. Only by risking victimizing himself by his resistive participation in cyclic nature (neither seeking to transcend it nor accepting conventionalized definitions of its potency) can he hope to discover within himself means for transfiguring the conditions giving rise to his discovering power.

"The Triumph of Life" was broken off by Shelley's unexpected drowning. We cannot be certain how, ultimately, he might have dramatized an alternative to the intolerable consequences of enlightened skepticism that was the source of his intellectual power, or exactly how his self-criticizing persona might have profited from Rousseau's darkly illuminating self-disfigurement. But it is clear that Shelley's vision does not include a transcendent power. Whatever can free us from enslavement to a condition of life that is no more than meaningless repetitions must be an achievement of purely "natural" human beings. So, like Wordsworth, Shelley engages himself, and us, in rethinking what "nature" may be. As various "visions" within the dream vision make plain, his poem of liberative self-reflection originates in a natural capacity for imagining. Inadequate imagining, however, may reenslave us within another delusional misconception of "the nature of things." Escape from such self-enslavement depends (paradoxically from any conventional religious perspective) on a continual reconceiving of how we can refigure the natural conditions out of which imaginative self-consciousness and its derivative sociocultural constructs have originated.

Shelley rejected the idea of a transcendent God. He also came to reject the Enlightenment replacement of God with "natural laws," which in fact too readily turn into metanatural principles, whose "metanaturality" merely images some particular scientific philosopher's unrecognized impulses and desires—his or her "false consciousness," as it were. Resistance to such unwitting metaphysical substitutes for transcendent explanations brings antagonistic Malthus and Shelley surprisingly close together. Both, for example, perceived danger in Enlightenment-based utopianist assumptions that the natural world operates according to principles congenial to the idealists' preconceptions about what is simply and perspicuously "reasonable," and therefore beneficial, to humanity. Malthus was content to display the self-contradictions of the Enlightenment's "reasonable" idealisms. Shelley, more radical (because he was committed to a more liberally enlightened "naturalism"), contested as inadequate the concept of "reason" upon which were founded Enlightened ideologies. He perceived the "reasonable basis" of these ideologies as dependent upon oversimplified conceptions of "nature." As conceived by

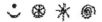

Enlightenment thinkers, our "natural reason" enables us to understand things (including our own minds) as they are, the machine as given and immutable, to make sense of what we have, or could have, already apprehended. The strength of such reasoning lies in its "realism," its ability to explain existent facts of nature, including human nature as we have come to understand it.

Some other power, however, is needed if all "facts" of nature are mutable, especially if they can be changed by human minds; if perception, as well as memory, is partially creative; if, as Emerson was to say, "perception makes." Shelley understood that if humans were unable to reconstruct nature significantly, the so-called creations of culture could not essentially differ from constructs of other social animals, such as termites. Shelley identified humankind's unique power to transform nature into culture with imagination, a mental capacity to think beyond what has existed and does exist, to establish, as he said, "heretofore unapprehended relations." Imagination can thus liberate us from the prison of immediate sensations—while remaining a purely natural power. There is nothing any more divine or mystical about imagining than reasoning or dreaming. Like dreaming, imagining does not accept the unalterability of things—including the mind's capacities—as they are currently known to be. Imagination refigures reality, and not just our figurations of reality as does dreaming. Acts of the human imagination can modify both internal-psychic and external-physical nature.

"The Triumph of Life" is, therefore, finally, most tantalizing in pointing toward the possibility of a biologically materialistic explanation of how the human mind works in processing perceptions, exploiting memory, developing language, and evolving rational and imaginative systems. In Shelley's day there was, of course, no scientific basis for articulating such an understanding. Today, as I hope my final chapter demonstrates, probably the most sophisticated scientific explanation of the brain's neuronal functioning is congruent with Shelley's speculations. His anticipation of discoveries made possible by scientific advances in biology is not mere chance. Shelley's ideas originate in conceptions of nature as an interplay of mutable systems, conceptions that are the matrix of evolutionary thinking. Edelman's theory of neural process in brain functioning is evolutionary, which is why he calls it Neural Darwinism. In fact, contemporary ideas of evolution in some respects modify Charles Darwin's conception along lines that pick up suggestions and approaches articulated by Darwin's romantic predecessors, such contemporaries of Shelley as Lamarck and Erasmus Darwin.[13]

It is necessary to emphasize how relatively little and how uncertain was the scientific support in the romantic age for the poets' proto-ecological views. Nowadays it is easy for even literary critics to pay casual lip service to ecological ideas. In the early nineteenth century to think of nature as the romantic poets did required an originality that we ought not to undervalue. This is why even Shelley, despite his idealism and hopefulness, was tempted toward Platonic and neo-Platonic escapes from naturalism. It is conceivable that his final poem would have ended at least as ambivalently as his prophetically hopeful propaganda-play *Hellas*.

> The world's great age begins anew,
> The golden years return,
> The earth doth like a snake renew
> Her winter weeds outworn;
> Heaven smiles, and faiths and empires gleam
> Like wrecks of a dissolving dream.
> . . . .
> O cease! must hate and death return?
> Cease! must men kill and die?
> Cease! drain not to its dregs the urn
> Of bitter prophecy.
> The world is weary of the past,
> O might it die or rest at last!
>
> (438–40)

At other times Shelley thought, however, that he could discern in social history concrete testimony to the transfiguring power of imaginative acts. The quality of such acts is revealed by his most characteristic and original imagery, which consistently relies on physical or material representations of psychic activity, or the reverse, the representation of physical phenomena through metaphors drawn from psychological processes. The superimposed similes that are perhaps the most idiosyncratic feature of his verse,[14] for instance, manifest the fluid continuousness that not only William James but also contemporary neuroscientists identify as essential

to the activity of consciousness. In "The Triumph" Rousseau describes, for a single example, how his original vision of the "shape all light" is superseded by the glaring brilliance heralding the car of life:

> And suddenly my brain became as sand
>
> Where the first wave had more than half erased
> The track of deer on desert Labrador,
> Whilst the fierce wolf from which they fled amazed
>
> Leaves his stamp visibly upon the shore
> Until the second bursts—so on my sight
> Burst a new Vision never seen before—
>
> (405–11)[15]

The characteristic difficulty of these lines arises because, although our minds do in fact operate thus fluidly, we are unaccustomed to linguistic representations of that continuous transformativeness. Shelley's verses are arranged, furthermore, so that, even as we recognize that the comparisons describe how Rousseau's mind processed in-pouring sensations, we simultaneously perceive that our own mind is constantly engaged in the same processing—indeed, is so functioning as we interpret these lines. Passages such as this, which abound in Shelley's verse, justify G. Kim Blank's observation that Shelley pushes the limits of linguistic capability farther than any other English poet. The poet's linguistic innovativeness is perhaps most simply suggested by his poem's disturbing title.[16] Not only is the conventionally exultant connotation of "triumph" inverted but the inversion is linked to what we most value, "life." As Tilottima Rajan argues, Shelley is forced to reconstruct accepted language deconstructively, because only if he can compel his readers to reconceive their crippling misconceptions can he inspire them to a truer understanding of human nature—and its best relations with an environment capable of fostering social liberty and personal pleasure.

In the next chapter I shall return to Shelley's poetry to articulate a little more fully his struggles with the consequences of this "naturalism" that intensified and complicated Wordsworth's Enlightenment-based counter-

Enlightenment intuitions. But an understanding of the context in which Shelley worked as the chief emulator-opponent of Wordsworthianism may at this point be clarified by glancing at Byron's confronting of the religious climate within which any changes in the idea of "nature" had to be carried out during the post-Napoleonic era. Byron's sensitivity to the religious overtones created by the sociopolitical conflicts of his age have consistently been underestimated. His knowledge of the Bible is matched among the romantic poets only by Blake. Shelley's verse displays superior familiarity with Greek literature, but it lacks the biblical allusions that saturate Byron's poetry. This difference reflects the difference in their reactions to what they both perceived as Wordsworth's political "apostasy." Shelley tends to condemn his predecessor's retreat into political reaction as grounded in an abandonment of his early "naturalism," whereas Byron is more likely to connect Wordsworth's political conservatism with a retreat into religious orthodoxy.

Byron was always alert to interconnections between religion and politics, as even his early "Turkish Tales" reveal. When in the early 1820s he began to focus his satiric attacks on the primary class of English readership that had earlier made him a celebrity, he centered his critiques on junction points of orthodoxy and political reaction, the kind of convergence embodied in conservative British governments' disposition to link sedition and blasphemy.[17] Blasphemy for modern critics has become a meaningless term, but in the early nineteenth century it could be the more damaging accusation. What makes Byron's experiments in biblical dramatization peculiarly interesting is his adopting a "radical" position antithetical to the sophisticated "higher criticism" in his era spreading from Germany into England.[18] Byron assumes the role of someone who takes the Bible literally. He offers no explanations founded on reference to the historical circumstances of scribes or prophets, dramatizing his "blasphemousness" by ostentatiously striking the pose of an accurate literalist.

What makes possible this pose in *Cain* is, paradoxically, the complex literariness of the drama, evidence that Byron in his own way is concerned with some of the same problems that preoccupied Keats and Shelley in their dream visions.[19] In the preface to *Cain: A Mystery*, published only a couple of years before his death, Byron defends his subtitle by citing medieval "mysteries or moralities" as prototypes. His adaptation of the

pre-Renaissance form to retell one of the Bible's most famous incidents seems part of a challenge to the Christianity espoused in *Paradise Lost*. A year or two before, in *The Vision of Judgment*, Byron had utilized a parodic "vision" to make fun of Milton's epic while savaging Robert Southey. In *Cain* he bypasses the laureate he loathed in order to subvert more seriously the Christian beliefs of which Milton's poem was by critical consensus esteemed the grandest exposition in English literature. Byron's "revisions" of the Bible are adequately understood only when we recognize them to be simultaneously critiques of Milton's epic. In *Cain* as in *The Vision of Judgment* Byron speaks to the moral condition of his times by undermining positions given special prominence by the creator of England's great Christian epic. Thus the famous Miltonic consolation in *Paradise Lost* of "A paradise within thee, happier far" (12.587) is ironically echoed in Byron's play by Lucifer, who advises Cain,

> Think and endure and form an inner world
> In your own bosom, where the outward fails.
>
> (2.2.463–64)

Not only the sophistry of Milton's *felix culpa* but its underlying division of "inner" and "outer" is thus challenged by Byron's materialistic "naturalism."[20]

Byron's chief purpose, however, appears to be to ensure that his readers do not fail to perceive the dark consequences of rejecting the Miltonic position. As Peter Thorslev has argued, Byron works in the spirit of Pierre Bayle to offer something more complex than another enlightened exposé of the evils of superstitious Christianity.[21] By deploying subversive references to *Paradise Lost* throughout *Cain*, Byron reveals dangers inherent in founding any ideological system upon dogmatic metacultural assumptions. The play's intriguing complexities, however, arise from Byron's awareness that rejection of Christian myth is likely to produce an unconscious mirror opposite, an explanation dependent upon disguised transcendental presuppositions. "God" all too easily reenters scientifically utopianist projects masquerading as "the nature of things," "instinctual drives," or "historical necessity."

This is why *Cain* begins with the punning stage direction "The Land without Paradise." Cain was the first man for whom God's beneficence could be no more than hypothesis or hearsay unconfirmed by the falling out of earthly affairs.

> One answer to all [my] questions, " 'Twas *his* will
> And he is good. How know I that? Because
> He is all pow'rful, must all good, too, follow?
> I judge but by the fruits—and they are bitter—
>
> (1.1.75–78)

Yet Byron's Cain refuses to subject his mind to what presents itself as true just because undivine, "God's" opposite, represented by the scientifically oriented Lucifer-Satan, who claims that Cain's skepticism toward God makes Cain Lucifer's worshiper:

> *Lucifer*: He who bows not to him has bow'd to me!
> *Cain*: But I will bend to neither.
>
> (1.1.317–18)

Cain's anguish, and his impressiveness, derives from his denial of this symmetric "me good, him bad" oppositionalism, his refusal to give up his resistance to any explanation that does away with all the inexplicably contradictory features of empirical experience. Paradise he never saw, but Cain is given by Lucifer ocular proof of pre-Adamic creatures in a cosmic pageant of Cuvierianian paleozoology, including "Intelligent, good, great, and glorious" humanlike beings (2.2.68). That demonstration is Lucifer's chief activity in this drama, because Light-Bringer-as-catastrophist showing natural creatures, animal and humanoid, that preexisted paradise dramatizes the central challenge to traditional Christianity posed by modern science. Since Cuvier was a celebrated proponent of "catastrophic" as opposed to gradualist "uniformitarian" earth historians, Lucifer's embodying of the French scientist's speculations evokes some of the same implications as Keats's depiction of Olympians suddenly superseding Titans. Both *Hyperion* and *Cain* represent a cosmos not chaotic but punctuated by unpredictably revolutionary events. If Cain is unpersuaded by his parents of God's providential goodness, the processes of natural history offer him no satisfactory alternative, even though he is dazzled by the beauty of the natural universe (2.2.241–45).

Cain rejects Lucifer's preference for sublimity over beauty along with his demand that Cain must choose between knowledge and love. This conflict of either/or versus both/and articulates Byron's insight into the dangerous ways in which "naturalism" may encourage us to evade rather than confront the moral problems that were justly the focus of a Christianity that no longer seems relevant. Even as Lucifer reinforces Cain's skepticism as to the validity of his parents' belief, the tempter inadvertently strengthens Cain's resistance to his own simplifying negativism. Cain is determined to rely on the experience of his senses, his affections and passions, and his relentlessly questioning intellect, even though these lead to no singular truth. The value of his determination is brought to the ultimate test when it, not Lucifer, leads him to murder his brother.

The murder occurs—significantly—after the issue of incest in the form of sexual love of siblings has been brought to the fore. Cain and his wife (here named Adah) were of course brother and sister. When Adah is shocked that their love could be considered sinful, Lucifer tells her that it is not so now, but it will come to be so regarded (1.1.363–4). Although the myth of a "universal" incest taboo had not in Byron's day yet been invented by anxious Victorian anthropologists and psychologists, through Adah's bewilderment the poet dramatizes how cultural history shapes our conceptions of what is "natural" or "unnatural." Her mystified, incomplete response—

> Can circumstance make sin
> Or virtue? If it doth, we are the slaves
> Of—
>
> (1.1.380–82)

lays the foundation for Cain's forebodings as to the fate of his infant son, Enoch. Cain, father as well as son and brother, goes so far as to conceive of destroying his child, observing, like the Sophoclean chorus, "better that he ceased to live," because

> so much of sorrow as he must
> Endure and, harder still, bequeath; . . .
>
> (3.1.133–34)

That Cain nevertheless blesses his son intensifies the irony that it is the heritage of his own act that Enoch will have to endure. This familial and historicizing perspective explains the significance of Byron's representation of the original murder in such stark contrast to Freud's imagining in *Moses and Monotheism* of sons' primal killing of the father of a primitive horde to get at his warehoused women as the origin of historical culture.[22] Byron dramatizes the fratricidal beginning of history as "anthropologically"—not psychologically or instinctually—motivated. Although the influence of sibling rivalry is not entirely dismissed, the dominant impulse of murder springs from the ceremony of the brothers' sacrificial offerings.

Abel kills animals and burns their flesh, whereas Cain, a farmer, offers grains and fruits. Given Byron's historicizing of the first human family's life outside paradise, the difference delineates contrastive fashions of constructing culture out of nature. The bias built into the drama compels us to look askance at the bloody basis of Abel's construct, presenting its violence as—ironically—the immediate cause of Cain's murderous blow, the first human blood-sacrifice. Fratricide thus is made to seem a product of "cultural" antagonisms in how to utilize the natural environment—meat-roasting herdsman opposing vegetarian farmer.

Cain treats the murder as one that might not have taken place. The killing appears, this is to say, as a fully *historical* act—indeed, *the* act that initiates human history as a story of contingent violences. The murder Byron portrays was not in any way necessitated, not made inevitable by either metaphysical system or some inner compulsion of precultural "human nature." *Cain* is as hostile to (yet unarticulated) Freudian dogmas as to (then) familiar Christian platitudes. Many critics today might be happier with Byron's protagonist were his fratricide presented as metahistorical—not a matter of religion, to be sure, but one of universal instinctual psychology. Surprisingly few objections, at any rate, have been raised against Freud's antithetical representation of the irresistible power of libidinal instincts in his primal drama of sons murdering their father, although this pseudoanthropological "re-creation" is implausible to the point of absurdity. Necessarily: a primal scene is not by definition a historical event.

Because *Cain* refuses to explain the history that it initiates in terms of supracultural psychological drives any more than by predestination or prov-

identiality, ambivalence becomes the only appropriate—however unsettling—response to this reimagining of the first murder. Byron's designation of his drama as a "mystery" thus finally seems paradoxically justified in demonstrating that the romantic proto-ecological vision is no simple substitute for traditional religion. The play instead focuses the disturbing uncertainty at the core of romantic rethinking of what nature consists, a reassessment that refuses either to deny absolutely any possibility of "spiritual" dimensions or the potential horror of a purely "natural" cosmos. It is exactly this uncertainty that encourages examination of the incontrovertibly material conditions of our intrinsic ethical insecurity. Every part of *Cain,* not just its Cuverian episode, represents the ground for cultural accomplishment as proactive engagement with the physical cosmos in both its sinister grandeurs and its specific, evanescent lovelinesses. Byron's "mystery" enables us, then, to describe schematically primary causes of the special romantic fascination with natural phenomena. Natural history and human history, however different, are inextricably intertwined; so far as we misunderstand the former, our conception of the latter will be defective. The possibility of ecology therefore appears when humankind becomes competent ("negatively capable," in Keatsian language) to accept nature's transformative multiplicity as the essential basis for valuable but not absolute cultural constructs and ceases trying to oversimplify natural processes by imposing on them reductively metanatural fantasies, even those representing themselves as "scientifically" antifantastic.

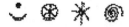

eight

Shelley: The Socialization of Mind

The primal paradox in the life and thought of Percy Shelley is that, although steeped in the ethos of the Enlightenment, he came to perceive Enlightenment thinking as delusional, especially in its definitions of humankind's appropriate relations to the natural world. The paradox echoes in Shelley's polemical representations of Wordsworth as a self-betrayer, because Shelley's verse persistently betrays the painful intensity of his responsiveness to Wordsworth's innovations in what used to be called "nature poetry." Perhaps the decisive emulative antagonism between the poets appears in the "main haunt and chief region" of their songs, "the mind of Man." The elder poet celebrates mind in its individuality; to the younger, the human mind is fascinating as the fundamental medium of socialization.

The difference is the driving force of the "Ode to the West Wind." This is perhaps Shelley's best-known poem, by several leading Shelleyans treated as his supreme accomplishment, a dazzling display of his subtly complex technical skills. The praise has obscured the oddest thematic feature of the ode. Left unstated in this "prophetic ode" is what the poet would specifically prophesy.

Scatter, as from an unextinguished hearth
Ashes and sparks, my words among mankind!
Be through my lips to unawakened Earth
The trumpet of a prophecy.

(66–69)[1]

The message to be borne by the poet's words, however, remains unarticulated. Against the preferences of recent new historicists, Shelley foretells no utopian scheme. He prays only that his words may manifest how processes of external nature and processes of human imagining can be mutually reinforcing. The ode's famous final question therefore resonates as more than rhetorical: "If winter comes, can spring be far behind?" Why should a natural truism become an interrogative unless its metaphoric appropriateness is in doubt? Shelley prays that his speech be animated by what arouses the great seasonal destructive/preserving changes of sky, earth, and waters. A prayer built on such metaphor may, by emphasizing the metaphor, surreptitiously imply that the annual cycle of nature in fact differs from moral reawakening. Mankind "awakened" presumably would not be prisoners of nature's merely cyclic repetitiveness. Even the mighty, ocean-shaking power of the wind may, after all, be insufficient to image Shelley's cultural aspiration.

Here again a second-generation romantic poet revises his immediate predecessors' revisions of tradition. Coleridge in "France: An Ode" projects himself confidently from his cliff above the sea into vast forces of nature. Within them, rather than within a social community, he feels sure of finding "liberty." Shelley prays, inversely, for the "breath of autumn's being" to enter into him. The reversal requires Shelley to elaborate and to redeploy with intricate artistic and intensified "scientific" precision the relatively simple and traditional Coleridgean imagery of cloud, forest, and wave. Shelley foregrounds the consciousness of the poet making use for his own purposes of what is offered by processes of nature. His prayer ends interrogatively rather than exclamatorily, because in its very appeal to natural forces the poem questions their validity as a model for cultural regeneration. The emotional evocativeness of the ode springs from this dramatization of a fundamental imaginative conflict out of which every form of ideological consciousness must for Shelley be constructed: nature

121

as simultaneous model and antimodel for human aspiration. The poem thus recovers through a "scientific" understanding of the destroying/preserving wind something analogous to the original, prescientific potency of the concept of "inspiration." By the early nineteenth century, only by questioning the wisdom of founding human ideals on metaphors derived from natural forces could a power like that of "divine breath" any longer be usefully reconceived. Any political consciousness, moreover, is for Shelley false consciousness so far as it is not founded upon recognition that it, like every other idealism, is rooted in humankind's "naturalness," difficult to define because it is ever-changing.

Such prophetic skepticism toward traditional conceptions of nature as a source of ideological models explains the necessary ambivalence at the heart of all romantic "love" of nature. This love depends on awareness of the dangers of too simply taking an accepted understanding of "the natural" as a guide for human behavior, especially in imaginative projects.[2] Unless "nature," for example, is conceived as a complex of self-transformative processes interactively animating both external world and "human nature," appeals to the "natural" will inevitably contravene humankind's most humane aspirations. Shelley anathematizes accepting as a moral guide deceitful appearances of natural order that are in fact "anarchic." The purposeless and endlessly unprogressive cycle of the seasons, for example, is in itself finally no more than a spectacular display of the triumph of entropy, necessarily concluding in Buffon's vision of a frozen earth, a prospect that horrified Shelley as the remains of Javanese turtles horrified Schopenhauer.[3] To be valuable to man, "nature" must be conceivable as more than systems of repetitive regularity. The west wind must be acclimated within the imagining mind if it is to become the vehicle of any humanly significant "resurrection," that is, a revival that is more than cyclical repetition. In and of itself the west wind accomplishes nothing more than continuing a meaningless round of destroying and fertilizing, death using life to produce more dead bodies.

If Shelley's prayer is answered, however—if the wind does become the vehicle of his imagination—others, not the poet himself, will be the beneficiaries of what he breathes forth. This "selflessness" illustrates Shelley's shifting of the Wordsworthian concentration on autobiography toward psychosocial history. The shift is most dramatic in "The Mask of Anarchy," which foresees the possibility of a liberating change in the "popular"

mind. As I have earlier suggested, Shelley conceives of liberating political action as originating not in the inspiration of a "great" leader or in any specially "enlightened" class or group such as an intelligentsia but in an entire "people's" self-transformation of their inbred mental-emotional attitudes. This belief that each mind of those constituting "the masses" *can* be changed by itself communally, that "the people" can teach themselves as individuals to change what they have internalized, revolutionizes political theorizing to a degree that scholars are only today beginning to appreciate.

Shelley represents "the people" as behaving in a fashion that will improve their current circumstances by making creative use of past traditions. It is not very important whether the view of the beneficence of "Old England's" ways celebrated in "The Mask of Anarchy" is factually correct. What matters much more is Shelley's intellectually innovative consciousness that an attitude or mode of behavior long disused or fallen out of mind may be fruitfully revived to ameliorate new difficulties. This power of revival of human accomplishments long abandoned, forgotten, superseded, or concealed is fundamental to the peculiar capacity for learning that distinguishes humankind from all other social animals.[4] It is a power upon which the success of many complicated and significant social transformations depends.

A major cultural exemplification of such recovery in Shelley's day was the so-called Hellenistic revival.[5] As with the Renaissance of Roman classicism, with romantic Hellenism what had seemingly been permanently obliterated was self-consciously resurrected. In both instances, the direct continuity between distant past and present had been systematically denied. The "revival" therefore disrupted the disrupting cultural intervention. The revivers rejected the commitments of their immediate past, condemning them as intrusive or aberrant. When Shelley says, "We are all Greeks," he rejects not merely many centuries of Christianity but more particularly the romanized classicizing that had culminated in the eighteenth century. Such recoveries from the oblivion of cultural repressions—which derive from the distinctively human capacities for anachronism and archaism—may well be the most significant social manifestations of human consciousness. They are acts of which only creatures with culture are capable, a deliberate exploiting of facts of recognized discontinuity to produce new forms of reality. Other organisms are not only imprisoned within their immediate sensory environment but also restricted by unmitigated physical continuities to their immediate past. In human culture, natural vitality attains the capacity of functioning even through discontinuity.

The learning that implies the ability to recover what humanity or nature has made to vanish is the key to Shelley's use of history. His use is antagonistic to that of conservative political thinkers, of whom Edmund Burke may here be taken as a pertinent representative. Tradition for Burke exists as essentially a continuity. His traditionalism is that of adhering to practices, physical or mental, that can and should persist in their operations. He does not recommend investigation into a more distant past for the discovery of forgotten ways that might usefully be resurrected *against* continuing customary practices and ideas. His traditionalism is undialectical, distrustful of discontinuity, uninterested in the long vanished. Shelley, contrarily, happily presents radicalism as radical rediscovery. For him, social innovativeness may be developed and perfected by historical self-consciousness constructed out of reanimation of what has vanished or been forgotten or deliberately stamped out.

Such willingness to rediscover is accompanied by the typical romantic perception that a major feature of history is its manifestation of delusions, especially self-delusions. Wordsworth is the first poet to question the accuracy of his intense memories and to explore how we profitably change our memories.[6] But for all the romantics, including famously in this instance William Blake, the primary representative of noble, even inspiring, self-delusion was John Milton. The revered author of *Paradise Lost* was, in Blake's words, of the devil's party without knowing it. Shelley's formulation is more subtle but makes the identical point about *Paradise Lost*.

Milton's poem, he says, contains a philosophical refutation "of that system of which, by a strange and natural antithesis, it has been a chief popular support."[7] Such rejections of official Milton to redeem the concealed because self-misunderstood Milton intensify our appreciation for the broad significance of the romantic aspiration, not to escape from ambivalence but to become capable of achieving it. Milton's heroic poetry and political tribulations exercised a complex fascination for the romantic poets. Shelley's comment, for example, is ultimately complimentary. He implies, as does Blake, that, deep down, Milton was on the

"right" side. But more important, Milton exemplifies how we can learn from the past what the past did not and could not know of itself. To do this we must be willing to investigate it deconstructively. I use the modern term, because Shelley's interpretation is founded on a perception of how Milton's articulation of a hidden "truth" covertly contradicts what he overtly enunciates. Such contradictions and self-delusions make it possible for us to learn from the past through critical analyses. Awareness of the past's self-contradictions frees us from blind acceptance of the customary, so that we may innovate by means of what tradition has kept capable of resurrection by denying. Learning through such deconstructive reconstruction gives us the ground for reconceiving our own immediate situation, liberating ourselves from submission to both external and internalized unexamined preconceptions, freeing us to relate to the past in new ways. Whereupon, if we are successful, the old text that was our starting point may begin to radiate freshly inspiring ideas and perceptions.

Here I repeat my observation in the preceding chapter that Shelley (quite in contrast to modern deconstructionists) anticipates a biologically materialistic understanding of how the mind works. Virtually all his major poems foresee socially beneficent results from a harmonizing of mankind's inner psychic and nature's external physical processes. If we can but properly imagine materialistically both "mind" and "nature," we may hope to attain nontranscendent deconstructive reconstructions of cultural life for which the most beautiful of previous paradisal fantasies will seem faint and inadequate representations.

That *if*, of course, is a mega-*if*, as the intertwined dramas of *Prometheus Unbound* and *The Cenci* illustrate. Before examining the interlock between those visions of idealistic hope and realistic fear, however, it will be helpful to observe how an early lyric such as "Mont Blanc" tries to deepen into systematic principle Wordsworthian intuitions of a fittingness of interchanges between mental activity and physical processes of external nature. What makes Shelley's attempt so difficult is that he refuses to reduce the powerful indeterminacy that is the core of the young Wordsworth's intuitions. That indeterminacy is expressed in phrases such as "something far more deeply interfused" in "Tintern Abbey." The highly articulated structures evoked by Shelley's poem are equally undefinable in the conventional language of his day. The nontranscendent energy that is the key to the fit of human nature and external nature is experienceable and poetically describable, but given the historical development of English at the beginning of the nineteenth century, the fit cannot "reasonably" be explained, except by distorting it. In short, in representing their experiences with the natural world, the romantic poets *had* to write with new imaginativeness, which meant carrying language beyond then-acceptable limits.[8]

This in part explains the unusual form of "Mont Blanc," which uses an intricately disguised patterning of rhymes, for which the hidden model may be its metaphysical antithesis, Milton's "Lycidas."[9] So successfully disguised is Shelley's rhyming that some critics have discussed the poem as if it were written in blank verse—as is Coleridge's "Hymn before Sunrise in the Vale of Chamouni." The pretense of poetic composition in situ is also more overt in Coleridge's lyric, which is a paraphrase and elaboration of a work by the Swiss poetess Frederika Brun, not, like Shelley's poem, a response to actual visual experiences. The relevance of Coleridge's poem as thus an inspirational antimodel can hardly be exaggerated, as may be suggested by these early lines of Coleridge's effusion:

> O Sovran BLANC,
> The Arve and Arveiron at thy base
> Rave ceaselessly; but thou most awful Form!
> Risest from forth thy silent sea of pines,
> How silently!
> . . . .
> But when I look again,
> It is thine own calm home, thy crystal shrine,
> O dread and silent Mount! I gazed upon thee,
> Till thou, still present to the bodily sense,
> Didst vanish from my thought; entranced in prayer
> I worshipped the Invisible alone.[10]

We should understand Shelley's "Mont Blanc" as working revisionarily within this romantic convention (more successfully embodied in "Tintern Abbey") allowing the poem's words to appear as if addressed to the landscape it describes. This pseudoimmediacy, as I have already observed, opens the way to having the landscape "speak" for itself, allows a transposition of description into a dialogical lyricism. In "Mont Blanc" the

speaking landscape becomes both more paradoxical and more portentous than in most Wordsworthian lyrics, for through its silence, Shelley claims, the mountain can address with tremendous effect much more than the individual poet: "Thou hast a voice, great mountain, to repeal / Large codes of fraud and woe."

The social efficacy of this natural voice resides in its underlying silence, whose paradoxical strength is but feebly articulated in the deafening thunder of the Arve's cataracts and the grinding roar of its awesome glaciers. The oxymoron of silent voice, to be redeemed in the poem's final lines, extends and deepens the humanizing "fallacy" used by Wordsworth to bestow on natural landscape the power of "speaking" without encrustations of personifying conventions. In every way Shelley's poem intensifies the Wordsworthian literalized interactivity of mind and landscape. The generic situation delineated in the famous opening lines, for instance, is at once converted by "thus" into a simile for dramatizing the interpenetrating play between the Ravine of the Arve and the imagination of its spectator.

> Thus thou, Ravine of Arve—dark, deep Ravine—
> Thou many-coloured, many-voiced vale . . .
> . . . .
> Dizzy Ravine! and when I gaze on thee
> I seem as in a trance sublime and strange
> To muse on my own separate phantasy,
> My own, my human mind, which passively
> Now renders and receives fast influencings,
> Holding an unremitting interchange
> With the clear universe of things around;
> One legion of wild thoughts whose wandering wings
> Now float above thy darkness, and now rest
> Where that or thou are no unbidden guest,
> In the still cave of the witch Poesy,
> Seeking among the shadows that pass by
> Ghosts of all things that are, some shade of thee,
> Some phantom, some faint image; till the breast
> From which they fled recalls them, thou are there!
> (12–48)

This conversion into poetic figure of the stipulated fact of psychic-physical relationships (universe of things in mind, mind in universe of things) permits Shelley to work a simultaneous reconversion. Making use of an ambiguous antecedent, *that* in line 43 ("Where that or thou are no unbidden guest"), the poet displays the poetic imagination's transformative mobility as founded upon the presence *within* the mind of that "flow" of natural processes so stupendously manifested by the physical setting of Western Europe's greatest mountain.

Shelley chooses an almost anti-Wordsworthian scene of stark, Aeschylean grandeur because he is not principally concerned with private experience. His focus is on the understanding of sociohistorical processes in the light of new conceivings of the relationship of human beings to the physical world. What the poet looks at is no familiar, lovely landscape but manifestations of the desolate destructiveness of catastrophic geologic forces that are, nonetheless, the "breath and blood of distant lands." In that contradiction the vital potency of the "flow of things" stands boldly revealed. The poem's final revelation, however, is that this power of earth is also our power, mankind's power. This poem's concluding question, like that of the "Ode to the West Wind," is not merely rhetorical. It implies that silence and solitude, primal attributes of power per se, are not "vacancy" to "the human mind's imaginings." The enclosed implication is that without such imaginings silence and solitude would be vacuous. That is, they would be only what they are physically: negation, absence, isolation—what is incomprehensible to us because it renders impossible any "unremitting interchange" between human mind and natural world.[11]

What the motionless poet perceives in the static mountain is that power exercised is mobility and evanescence, both in physical and in human nature. The enduring principle of the universe, in contemporary terms, is energy. True being, therefore, is mutability, not stasis. The fulfillment of human nature, not as mere personal experience but as realized in social experience, comes through its living interchange of energies with the "universe of things around," accepting them within our imagination even as it penetrates their deceptive exteriority. So far as we sustain this vital interdependence, humankind empowers, even as it is empowered by, nature.

Almost a figuration of this interchange appears in the intertwining compositional histories of *Prometheus Unbound* and *The Cenci*, counterdramas

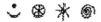

exploring the terrible wonder of simultaneously revering and suspecting ourselves as we were admonished to do in Wordsworth's "Lines Left upon a Seat."[12] Prometheus, lyrically hopeful, teaches how we may learn to exercise these dual capacities; *The Cenci* dramatizes with grim irony the difficulty of so learning. For Shelley, any poem's success at "educating the human heart through its sympathies and antipathies," as the preface to *Prometheus Unbound* explains, requires that it attain a peculiar autonomy through engagement with the creations of previous and contemporary poets. As in his *Defence of Poetry*, Shelley presents himself in this preface as inspired to insights into human nature and the nature of the cosmos by his participation in the communal event of an imaginative efflorescence of his cultural epoch: "The great writers of our own age are . . . the companions and forerunners of some unimagined change in our social condition or the opinions which cement it. The cloud of mind is discharging its collected lightning." In place of the singular oedipal conflict by which contemporary critics like Harold Bloom define relations between poets, Shelley depicts the relationships in terms of an interchanging mutuality in images drawn from the operations of physical nature, insisting that "a poet is the combined product of such internal powers as modify the nature of others, and of such external influences as excite and sustain these powers; he is not one, but both. . . . Poets . . . are, in one sense, the creators, and in another, the creations, of their age" (135).[13]

An equivalent reciprocity keys the processes of emotionalized learning central to the two counterposed dramas of *Prometheus* and *The Cenci*. Such learning is the antithesis of compiling information. Shelley insists that he abhors "didactic poetry." What he seeks to teach and how he teaches is summarized in his description of his purpose in *The Cenci*:

> to familiarize the highly refined imagination of the more select classes of poetic readers with beautiful idealisms of moral excellence; aware that, until the mind can love, and admire, and trust, and hope, and endure, reasoned principles of moral conduct are seeds cast upon the highway of life which the unconscious passenger tramples to dust, although they would bear the harvest of his happiness. (135)

The key word in this passage is *until*. The romantic poet believes that we *learn* to love. The finest qualities of the human mind and spirit are acquired through examined experience, conscious training, continuous enhancements of our inborn proclivity to learn. This is why beauty (a term abandoned by recent criticism), particularly beauty of the natural world, is tremendously important to the romantics. Beauty draws forth our best powers and thus enables us consciously to improve the most valuable capabilities of our minds. These capabilities are for the exercise of reciprocal functions, engagements in mutuality, what Keats called "interassimilative" processes.

We ought to take seriously, then, a passage in the *Prometheus* preface often passed over casually.

> This Poem was chiefly written upon the mountainous ruins of the Baths of Caracalla, among the flowery glades and thickets of oderiferous blossoming trees, which are extended in ever widening labyrinths upon its immense platforms and dizzy arches suspended in the air. The bright blue sky of Rome, and the effect of the vigorous awakening spring in that divinest climate, and the new life with which it drenches the spirits even to intoxication, were the inspiration of this drama. (133)

Prometheus Unbound is, indeed, animated by a vision of natural life reborn out of the mind-polluting desolations of imperialistic tyranny. As we have learned, however, from romantic poem after romantic poem, from " A Slumber Did My Spirit Seal" to the "Ode to the West Wind," such a vision must take account of cosmic indifference and the fashion in which natural mechanisms are no valid model for human accomplishment.

Prometheus Unbound explores the insufficiency of the natural rebirth of spring as a tempting figure for the revitalizing of human minds. Shelley's choice of Prometheus as his protagonist is founded on a perception of the dangerous intricacy of the mind's "natural" workings. Prometheus is a figure superior, for Shelley's purposes, to Milton's Satan, who he says "engenders in the mind a pernicious casuistry which leads us to weigh his faults with his wrongs, and to excuse the former because the latter exceed all measure" (133). This is a "casuistry" equivalent to that the poet will attribute to observers who force themselves to excuse Beatrice Cenci. In both dramas Shelley extends Wordsworth's recognition that our minds all too readily injure themselves. The very power of the human mind assures that such injurious actions will easily become institutionalized. Distort-

ing self-injuries internalized by the inheritors of inadequate modes of thinking will lead these deluded legatees to regard their distorted views as authorized by "nature." So Prometheus's worst torment is his vision of Christ, because in him the Titan sees how goodness is by slavishness perverted in the very name of its source.

> I see, I see
> The Wise, the mild, the lofty, and the just,
> Whom thy slaves hate for being like to thee,
> (1.1.604–6)

Such "natural" perversions as Christians hating most those most like Christ explain why Shelley was drawn to represent mental actions by means of physical images, and physical processes by means of imagery "drawn from the operations of the human mind." His vision, especially at its most optimistic, is of the power of our consciousness as a naturally transfiguring but not transcending power. Our consciousness, if operating properly, binds us wonderfully, not disastrously, to the natural world. The mind can find the natural world "beautiful," because that is where the human mind works best. So *Prometheus Unbound*, perhaps Shelley's poem most profoundly concerned with internal psychic states, simultaneously overflows with descriptions of beautiful natural scenes.

This combination is the core of the play's dramatically "undramatic" structure. As most commentators have observed, dramatic action in the usual sense is finished in the beginning of the first act when Prometheus "recalls" his curse of Jupiter. This act of forgiveness, however, initiates the transformation of the natural world and humankind, the unfolding of which revitalization occupies all the rest of the drama. Two points need to be made about this surprising organization of what Shelley calls a "lyrical drama." First, *The Cenci*, written concurrently, proves that Shelley was quite capable of writing a play built upon "conventional" dramatic action. The true "drama" of *Prometheus Unbound* lies in its reversing of dramaturgical conventions and expectations. Second, this drama of deliberate form-reversal is expressive of Shelley's belief that beneficial psychic change can (indeed must) change the natural world.

He so believes because for him the human mind is a natural power that exists through its interactivity with other natural powers. Nature is important to us, and we are important to nature, because our self-consciousness is part of material evolutionary processes. Prometheus shows us how we make the earth a cursed place or a paradise because it is *our* proper dwelling place, the place wherein we find our happiness, or not at all.

That Wordsworth's assertion is the "message" of Shelley's play appears when one sketches the outline of the undramatically dramatic situation that *Prometheus Unbound* elaborates. The mother of Prometheus, whose name means forethought or foretelling, is earth, as she tells him:

> I am the earth
> Thy mother, she within whose stony veins
> To the last fibres of the loftiest tree
> Whose thin leaves trembled in the frozen air
> Joy ran, as blood within a living frame,
> When thou didst from her bosom, like a cloud
> Of glory arise, a spirit of keen joy!
>
> (1.1.152–58)

Promethean forethought developed a marvelous world until power over it was usurped by Jupiter, a creation of Prometheus. Jupiter chained Prometheus to an icy mountain and subjected him to ceaseless tortures because he would not reveal to Jupiter his knowledge of how the tyrant's reign would be terminated. This dramatizes how institutionalizing corrupts: those empowered by institutions become preoccupied solely with retaining power for its own sake, which makes power meaningless, lacking in purpose. Prometheus finally recalls the curse he directed at Jupiter when he was first imprisoned by his creature. This act arouses Asia, his separated love, to journey to the cave of Demogorgon, a mysterious power that rises and easily overthrows Jupiter (because "he" is nothing more than a phantasm, a "conception" of Prometheus), thereby freeing Prometheus and reuniting him with Asia. Their reunion transforms the earth into a delightful place of fecund beauty and vitality in which human societies flourish, at least for a time, in idyllic freedom.

I rehearse this radical revision of Aeschylus's severe agon, because some central significances stand out boldly when one looks at its skeletal peculiarities. In the first place, when Prometheus changes his mind, the con-

dition of the earth changes. The change is not merely of perception. Real phenomenal conditions alter. Shelley has dramatized what in chaos theory is called initial condition dependence. Some recent critics view Prometheus's act of forgiveness as a "mere" shift in perspective or point of view. The forgiveness of Jupiter that Prometheus enunciates, however, is a drastic psychic reversal of attitudes, feelings, ideas. To give up hating an object and to begin pitying it is to reorder one's personality radically. There is, in truth, no more "revolutionary" psychological act than an act of forgiveness, but its power lies in its superficially "undramatic"—even antidramatic—character. It is a reversal of inner life whose potency usually can be manifested only in external actions that will appear in conventional terms "weak." So in Shelley's play, earth, anticipating Nietzsche, believes that Prometheus's forgiveness is a signal of moral feebleness, when in fact he has begun earth's—his mother's—revival. His act and her misunderstanding aptly dramatize the biological relation of self-consciousness to its originating matrix.

Prometheus disavows his curse of Jupiter by having it repeated back to him by a "phantasm" of Jupiter. One effect of this, of course, is to show "Jupiter" to be a manifestation of Prometheus's unacknowledged fear and hate. When Prometheus "forgives" Jupiter, he admits *his* capacity to injure, thereby exorcizing the self-torturing aspect of his mind. Jupiter, one might say, is Prometheus's—Forethought's—propensity to self-tyranny. "Our most dreadful enemy," we may recall Wordsworth warning us, are "our pre-established codes of decision," the most dangerous of Shelley's "codes of fraud and woe." It is not impulse but forethought that devastates the natural world and makes human societies hell. It is not thoughtlessness but deliberate planning (we will cut down those trees to build that mall, we will bomb those bastards) that pollutes the earth and populates it with human beings determined to kill and starve each other. The Zeus-subsuming imperialism of Roman Jupiter, Shelley's names remind us, originated in the liberating Greek imagination.[14]

Prometheus embodies self-consciousness as a natural phenomenon manifesting the emergence of culture from material nature. Prometheus first undergoes tortures in the savagery of icy mountains, empty of life—pierced by "crawling" glaciers' "spears / Of their moon-freezing crystals." The epithalamic fourth act functions as a lyrical perepeteia of this frozen barrenness, reinforcing the representation of "Jupiterism" as blind resistance to mutability. Shelley, like Byron, stresses Prometheus's power of endurance, but the romantic Titan endures not merely to display stoical firmness but *for* change, to make transformativeness possible. Shelley represents the everlasting potentiality for self-alteration of natural being in Demogorgon, whose terrific power manifests not humankind's alienation from cosmic systems but how these are means for the fullest realization of the capabilities of our consciousness. This is why the texture of the lyric drama must be woven out of the interassimilative relations of external phenomena and processes of mental activities, as in the celebrated sphere passage (4.236–61). The beauty of these relations is foretold in the words of the dream that leads Asia to the cave of Demogorgon (2.1.143–53), then given reciprocal embodiment in the spectacular sunrise experience on the mountain peak from which Asia and Panthea descend to Demogorgon's cave. The aural climax to this vision comes in the form of a simile comparing the "sun-awakened avalanche" to the terrific effects upon human societies of the sudden release of some "great truth" (2.3.18–42),[15] a comparison epitomizing Shelley's consistent dramatizing of the materiality of ideational processes.

If the beauties of *Prometheus Unbound* figure forth how self-reverence means reverence for ourselves as natural beings, *The Cenci* is *Prometheus*'s mirror opposite in urging us to suspect these wonderful capacities, because the central issues are the same as in the happier play. Beatrice is a tragic heroine, Shelley tells us in his preface to this drama, because she was unable to forgive her father. She was mistaken to take revenge on her repulsive parent who wished to murder his sons and who incestuously raped her and attempted to brutalize her mind. When I teach the play to undergraduates, a majority in each class say at once that the playwright is unjust to Beatrice.[16] Some students engage in the casuistry against which Shelley warns in his preface—"the restless and anatomizing casuistry with which men seek the justification of Beatrice, yet feel that she has done what needs justification" (240). Many simply think that a father who behaves as Count Cenci does deserves to be killed by his daughter—or by anybody else who happens along. By the time we have finished discussing the play, however, almost all these students have rethought their original position and revised, usually with some discomfort, their spontaneous and not unadmirable immediate emotional reactions.

I bring forward this evidence of the ethical complexity of *The Cenci*

because my concern with the play here compels me to pass over important sociopsychological issues it raises—such as the patriarchal silencing of women. I wish to focus attention on the drama's counter-*Prometheus* dramatizing of the hazards of self-consciousness, above all its potentiality to destroy self-reverence. The decisive turning point exactly at the midpoint of the tragedy is Beatrice's struggle with herself to decide what she should do in response to her father's brutal actions.[17] Rejecting suicide as a sin, she decides that the revengeful murder of her father is not only justified but a moral imperative.

Shelley's representation of her arrival at this determination compels us to recognize her disturbing temperamental similarity to her father. Just as his incestuous rape is not an act of impulsive passion, so her plan to murder him is coldly calculated. Both characters are in this respect Promethean: both are forethinkers. The appalling power of the violence in *The Cenci* arises not from passions unleashed but from the manipulation of emotions by "logical" reasoners, skillful planners, adept at justifying their actions through distortions of the language by which their society perpetuates its tyrannous systems.

Given the sociopolitical context established by the play, the protagonists' adroit reasoning is crucial. Shelley portrays the horror of modern oppressive ideologies, communism and fascism being leading exemplars for us, as stemming from perversely systematic rationality: their murders and suppressions are rooted in principle, are cold-blooded. *The Cenci* as mirror inversion of *Prometheus Unbound* exposes the psychic foundations of such ideological monstrousness. We delude ourselves into "Jupiterism" through failures of self-reverence originating in the very potency of our self-consciousness. Orsino, himself a morally slimy hypocrite, describes the Cencian trait of conscious self-analysis and its dangers.

> It fortunately serves my close designs
> That 'tis a trick of this same family
> To analyze their own and other minds.
> Such self-anatomy shall teach the will
> Dangerous secrets: for it tempts our powers,
> Knowing what must be thought, and may be done,
> Into the depth of darkest purposes: . . .
>
> (2.107–13)

What must be thought and may be done—seldom have the imperative and conditional been more illuminatingly juxtaposed. Murderous revenge upon her father inevitably occurs to Beatrice as a possible course of action. Her mistake is turning the possibility into an imperative. By so doing she makes herself truly her father's daughter. Considering the matter within herself, she reaches the conclusion that she has no choice. Any normal person will sympathize with the tortured, isolated girl's feelings that provoke her decision. Yet, as Shelley asserts in his preface, the terrible truth is that she would have been a better person had she been able to forgive her father. Yet how, my students ask, could she be expected to do that? In so asking, of course, they tend toward her judgment that in fact she has no choice—that, in short, she *must* give up (consciously!) the primary power of consciousness, the capacity to choose among alternatives.

The grounds for Shelley's claim that we ought not to degrade ourselves into creatures of choiceless instinct is by Prometheus's forgiveness of Jupiter presented as a recognition that Jupiter manifests qualities in Prometheus: real evil is never something merely other but also that of which we ourselves are capable. Beatrice in choosing murder revictimizes herself, just as Prometheus's tortures (he comes to realize) are the result of hate inside him. Beatrice represents herself to herself as one mercilessly enjoined to vengeance. To indulge in revenge is, of course, to bind oneself to a definition of relationship to one's victim that obliterates true personal choice. Revenge, as Aeschylus demonstrated and Hamlet understood, is all too reasonable a self-dehumanizing act.

Hamlet comes to mind because Beatrice arrives at her decision through self-communing, not through consultation and interchange with others, like her sympathetic stepmother. Here again she mirrors her father, who communicates with no one and remains confined within isolating self-analysis. She like her father denies herself the liberating possibility of evoking responses that may draw us into the realm of mutual responsibilities. Shelley makes it plain that as a woman and a daughter Beatrice is severely restricted in her ability to communicate—this, indeed, is a key oppression of her society, which reflects Shelley's negative judgment upon *his* society. But in noncommunicatively opting for revenge Beatrice "joins" in her society's conspiracy of silencing those it would keep powerless. She pays murderers to silence her father. Ironically, she and her family, however, are destroyed by verbal confessions of the

deed. They could have "saved" themselves, she claims, by remaining silent. This self-inverting irony underlines how, by committing herself to revenge, Beatrice has chosen to become what she hates. She thereby unwittingly helps empower the patriarchy that oppresses her—and all women. Ultimately she has silenced herself.

This harsh and difficult lesson should remind us how persistent is the romantic focus on self-betrayal. But looking at *The Cenci* in the context of *Prometheus Unbound*, we observe how tightly this preoccupation is bound into the romantic naturalistic conception of human self-consciousness. Beatrice fails in self-reverence. She does not admit her natural—not transcendent—capability to reconfigure her mind. She resists the possibility of altering herself—and of thereby altering her world. She becomes, finally, an extreme and more troubling development of Wordsworth's suicidal solitary. By her mode of "rejecting" her society's unfair and despicable systems of judgment, she destroys herself through making herself indistinguishable from what she so rightly hates.

Shelley's conception that Beatrice would have been wiser to behave toward her father as Prometheus finally does toward Jupiter springs from his faith that human beings are not trapped within a natural determinism, even though he believes in no transcendent God. Beatrice's God becomes, significantly, "Death," and her actions lead inevitably to her final vision of life as gruesomely meaningless. The tragedy of Shelley's play emerges from Beatrice's refusal to admit that human beings can change their minds. She is wrong. One *can* expel the tyrant in oneself by oneself, without divine intervention. We should recognize what must be thought: all of us have the potentiality to act as Count Cenci does. Admitting that we could be as monstrous as he is provides us with a "natural" basis for forgiveness. This in no way condones his acts; it merely offers us a genuine alternative. If we admit that we share the same impulses as the worst of men, we position ourselves to choose to act differently. Beatrice, however, prefers to remain within the compulsive cycle of vengeful violence to which her father has chained himself, accepting "life" as a way of making more dead bodies.

That introspection is her mode of arriving at this self-injury returns us to the characteristic romantic awareness of solipsism—ironically—as the great threat to the attainment of authentic individuality. For the romantics, the healthy self-conscious mind is an outgoing one. Love of nature can lead to love of man, because nature draws love out of us. Healthy self-consciousness is essentially responsive, boundary-crossing, interactive. In grim contrast to *Prometheus*, *The Cenci* is claustral, self-enfolded, entirely confined within architectural interiors instead of open nature, even its natural imagery tending toward "scorpions ringed by fire." It displays unnatural people, that is, people who denaturalize themselves.

Taken together, then, *Prometheus Unbound* and *The Cenci* demonstrate the critical mistake of trying to explain away or to ignore the romantic poets' persistent attention to humanity's relation to our natural surroundings. If we drop the bias of recent criticism, in fact, Shelley's intensifying of Wordsworth's principal intuitions will appear as an almost inevitable development from the personal toward the social. Wordsworth's profoundest discovery-creation was that we dehumanize ourselves most perniciously when we use our consciousness to separate ourselves from nature. The separation is disastrous because the natural environment is both the source and the primary sustainer of our singularly human power of consciousness, supremely manifested in our imagination. Because this creative capability of our minds is not transcendent, it is most fully realized when we use it to strengthen and reinforce our participative engagements with our natural environment, which, it was Shelley's task to insist, is primarily constituted by systems of human relationships, the patterns of our interactions with other people.

nine

Biology of Mind and the Future of Criticism

Are Shelley's thoughts about man's place in the cosmos ideas to which we should attend today? Because he is a proto-ecologist, should we dance in the street? No, but his poetry does enable us to think profitably about matters such as the "naturalness" of cultural accomplishments. Too many intellectuals still work from an assumption that nature and culture are essentially antagonistic. In an era of genetic engineering, that antithesis oversimplifies dangerously. What fascinated romantic Shelley, moreover, fascinates biologists and chemists today: understanding systems that underlie apparently unpatterned, seemingly random processes by which multifariously diversified and individualized organisms interact.

This kind of convergence is suggested by the thinking of Gaston Bachelard, whose attraction to Shelley's poetry I have already noted, who was lured into seeking links between scientific and poetic imagining by attention to mathematical approximation methods for the analysis of irrationals such as π that cannot be known precisely. "Approximate knowledge" that is always incomplete, open to modification, led Bachelard to conceive of consciousness as fundamentally an "open process," the structures of the human mind as necessarily changeable. Mary McAllester Jones thus summarizes his revision of Descartes's "I think therefore I am" as "I think therefore I evolve." This conception led Bachelard to regard poetic imagery as preeminently revealing humankind's relationship to the physical world of matter.[1]

The ecological criticism I am advocating asks that we examine poetry from a perspective that assumes the imaginative acts of cultural beings proffer valuable insights into how and why cultural and natural phenomena have interrelated and could more advantageously interrelate. This approach will help us to develop mutually enriching interconnections between humanistic and scientific modes of understanding humankind, the earth we inhabit, and their reciprocal interdependencies. Although such criticism is applicable to any writer of any period, the proto-ecological tendencies of the English romantic poets make them especially useful for beginning this project.

Such criticism is particularly needed now, in the last decade of the twentieth century. For too long literary critics have isolated themselves from scientific concerns and limited their thinking to an unnecessarily narrow range of metaphysical and ideological issues. One pernicious effect of this concentration has been the development of hermetic critical styles contemptuous of the generosities of nonspecialized intelligent discourse. In the past few decades, furthermore, the cumulative advance of scientific research has opened up extraordinarily exciting vistas in our understanding of the natural world and in our ability to influence and change—for good or ill—what previously had appeared an essentially "uncontrollable" and therefore "alien" nature. Given this circumstance, humanists whose primary concerns are the powers of human imagining could if they wished contribute much to the practical quality of life on this earth in the next century.

The globalized imagining I endorse, for example, would oppose the constrictive reductionism of politically correct critics who substitute for one dogmatic system its mirror opposite—for instance, substituting for imperialism anti-imperialism, or replacing a canon excluding female artists of color with a canon excluding white males. Such prolongations of a Cold War oppositionalist mentality is opposed by ecological thinking that tries to understand and define systems of interdependency. Ecological criticism, instead of studying works of literature in self-defensively exclusivist terms, nationalistic, ethnic, or ideological, seeks to discover each work's contribution to comprehensive possibilities of interactivity. The assumption underlying this search is that each work of art makes a

unique contribution to the success of human life conceived as composed of many cultures each multifariously constituted. Ecological criticism, in brief, would reestablish on every level the significance of diversity. The importance of diversity, and ultimately of uniqueness, has been threatened by recent postmodern separatist critics as seriously as by earlier modernist proponents of "universals"—which in fact turn out to be no more than generalizations of Western European modes of thought. Ecological criticism, rejecting the popular reductionism that goes no farther than "otherness," specifies the significance of concrete distinctions— thereby making possible a dynamically complex cosmopolitan vision capable of liberating criticism from endlessly subdividing itself into defensive parochialisms of spirit.

The roots of recent advances in scientific biology's comprehension of the astounding intricacies of natural life processes, advances whose anxieties and exhilarations equally evoke ecological criticism, may be traced back into the eighteenth century, when traditional mental separations of the natural from the human began to disintegrate, as humankind began to enable nature to "speak" with a new, and newly dangerous, intelligibility. The ambivalent play of discomfort with inspiration thus provoked has intensified over the past two centuries. An intriguing illustration of these origins is found in chemistry, for example, in the artificial segregation and identification of fundamental constituents, as in the analysis of "elemental" water into a combination of more primal hydrogen and oxygen. Some of the disturbing social resonances of such "progress" appear in Joseph Wright of Derby's celebrated painting *The Air Pump*. Vividly if melodramatically representing a popular demonstration encouraged by Priestly's discovery of oxygen, Wright's painting depicts a display of the effects of a vacuum on life through the death of a bird when air is exhausted from a glass bell enclosing it. Wright's central figure has been called a prototype of the "mad scientist." Certainly the demonstration within a domestic setting dramatizes the social (as well as physical) menace in progressive scientific experimentalism, its capacity through its most exciting discoveries to extinguish—invisibly—the very "breath of life."

Scientific progress has increased the need for more subtle and informed humanistic explorations than Wright's into the significance of humankind's developing consciousness of its interdependent relationship with our natural environment. Today we are likely to think of the threats

141

posed by our capacities to exploit nuclear power and genetic engineering. We ought not to forget that the latter evolved from nineteenth-century identifications of microscopic pathogenic organisms as the sources of disease, identifications that led to the development of vaccines. In these beneficent discoveries was involved already a reconfiguring of how human nature and external nature were related. Man and his environment, nature and culture, were then already becoming what needs to be described and understood, to return once again to Keats's word, interassimilatively, as mutually interactive participants in an ever–self-transforming set of interlocking systems. It is high time, therefore, that humanists again take up their responsibilities as informed students and commentators on the dynamics of humankind's relationship with the natural world.

One of the indubitable advances of literary criticism in recent years has been its breaking down of artificially rigid distinctions between texts and contexts. Ecological criticism would extend that tendency, in part by exploring how such fruitful dissolving of intellectually reductive boundary-inventing might be facilitated through awareness of ideas currently orienting the biological sciences. Some of the most impressive of these ideas underlie studies into the biological bases of human consciousness. Significant among such studies are those carried out and inspired by the Nobel Prize–winner Gerald M. Edelman. It will become apparent even from my awkward summary of his "Neural Darwinism" that such understanding of the physiological processes upon which human consciousness depends presents new ways of conceiving the interrelation of fundamental operations in culture-producing minds. Edelman's research seems to offer us a biologically materialistic understanding of mind, which I have suggested can be recognized as one goal of romantic thinking. This is more than a coincidence, because, as I have emphasized, the romantics conceived of nature along evolutionary lines, and the fundamental principle of Edelman's description of brain functioning is Darwinian selection.

Edelman's work, of course, has aroused debate and disagreement. Francis Crick, of DNA fame, for example, has raised objections to some of his ideas. Since Edelman emphatically denies that the brain is usefully described as a computer (the position of many "cognitivist" neuroscientists), he has encountered hostility from researchers committed to that

popular analogy. Some of this debate strikes an ignorant outsider like me as rather terminological, since the most recent computers seem different from the mechanistic, linearly oriented "Turing machines" developed by pioneers like von Neumann. Edelman himself makes extensive and imaginative use of computer modeling in his research to prove how uncomputerlike the brain. Because "Neural Darwinism" is controversial, however, I have founded my sketch of Edelman's position principally on his books *The Remembered Present: A Biological Theory of Consciousness* and *Neural Darwinism: The Theory of Neuronal Group Selection*, rather than *Bright Air, Brilliant Fire: On the Matter of the Mind*, which is directed toward more general audiences.[2] The value of Edelman's work on the brain (there is no dispute as to the brilliant innovativeness of his work on the immune system, for which he was awarded a Nobel prize) lies in his scientific work rather than in his, or my, efforts to popularize it. But I can say as a literary critic that both *Bright Air, Brilliant Fire* and *The Remembered Present*, although not easy books for a nonspecialist, are written with remarkable clarity and are admirable for the consistency of their attempts to make complex matters understandable to any intelligent reader.

The research underpinning Edelman's analysis of brain formations and brain structures that sustain human consciousness has revealed the embryonic development of the brain to consist of impressively variable processes. Development proceeds in a manner that assures unique patterns of connections between cells are established in each human brain. The brain, however, is not different in kind from all other organs in so developing. Analyzed carefully enough, every chicken feather turns out to be unique. This uniqueness of cell arrangement of every organ of every organism illustrates Darwin's assertion that populations of biological entities derive from systems of inheritance that do not merely allow but also foster diversity in a population. It is worth noting that contemporary biologists' discriminations on the cellular level extend the pioneering work of the great students of biology of the nineteenth century, such as Cuvier and Haeckel. These men perhaps most significantly advanced our understanding of the natural world by identifying systems of differentiation distinguishing species—Haeckel, as I have observed, having, for example, identified four thousand distinct kinds of *radiolaria* protozoa.

The survival value of variation within species resides, of course, in its equipping the species with possible means for responding successfully to changes in its environment. Variation in the cell arrangement in human brains serves this function in a specialized manner. Highly developed consciousness is a superlative means for enabling an organism to adapt rapidly to shifts, both local and global, in its environmental conditions— those conditions, of course, including the rest of the brain and the entire organism as well as events and conditions external to the organism.

How does this valuable power for variation occur in the brain? The brain in Edelman's view is composed not of preformed parts (like an unassembled motor) but of a huge population of relatively undifferentiated cells that in the process of development assume different specialized functions. The process at work is basically the same for the brain as for other parts of the body. Originally undifferentiated cells *develop* specialized characteristics, as one becomes a nerve cell, another a blood cell, a third a liver cell, and so on. How do they specialize? By joining a party, becoming a member of group, the blood group, the lung group, the nerve group. The cells join together primarily by means of their surfaces, on which in the course of the embryological process develop things like cell adhesion molecules and surface adhesion molecules. These possess varying degrees of stickiness. The variation of stickiness depends on where a cell happens to be at the time, say, that certain cell adhesion molecules develop, and how it happened to arrive at that position—in short, its history. The variations in stickiness determine which cells adhere to which, one might say n-stickiness becoming nerve cells, b-stickiness becoming blood cells, and so forth.

Exactly the same processes take place in the formation of the brain, key to which are neuron groupings that I shall refer to here as repertoires. These are joinings-together in different ways of cells according to the same historical processes of congenial stickiness that leads to the differentiation of other organs from one another. This means that the particular repertoires of each individual's brain, like the other organs of the body, are not directly controlled by the genetic code, the constraining instructions promulgated by the genes. Individual variation in each organ, including the brain's diverse repertoires, is an inevitable result of the historical process by which the organism as a whole and each of its parts comes into being embryologically. Genes in relation to particular cells and cell units are thus rather in the position of the parents of adolescents: although the parents are ultimately "responsible," and may perhaps set

certain limits of behavior, they have no immediate control over whom in particular their offspring hang out with, and so over how they "learn" to behave.

Developing cells stick together at their surfaces, or do not stick together, depending on the congeniality or antipathy of their adhesion molecules with those of the cells they happen to encounter at the historical moment that a particular specialization, or set of specializations, is taking place. If my understanding is correct, in all these procedures the brain develops according to the same natural processes as all the other organs. Everybody has a liver, but, examined closely, each human liver is unique, because each liver had a unique historical development. Everybody has a brain, but each is unique because each develops uniquely. The brain, however, is infinitely more complex than any other organ. Brains, indeed, are probably the most complex things on earth. The brain, to use Edelman's comparison, is smaller but more complex than a jungle. The individuality of every human being, therefore, is most apparent, and most importantly manifested, in its brain functionings.

The unique complexity of the brain, in fact, gives it the power of developing consciousness. That special power is the ultimate focus of Edelman's study. His work originated, significantly, not just from analysis of cell behavior and formation but also from study of observations about conscious behavior in animals. Consciousness wherever it appears, for example, is always continuous and successive. The continuity of consciousness is especially obvious in those animals with a richly developed nervous system—the brains of which show the most individual variation. Edelman's explanations of brain functioning consistently take into account this continuity, which not only is sequential in time but includes connectivity to the full spatiotemporal context of activities within which that temporal continuity exists. The context for any one brain function thus encompasses both the continuously changing operation of other brain functions as well as the continuous changes in the "outside" environment with which the brain engages. Edelman's explanations are always, therefore, holistic, temporally as well as spatially. A conscious brain is inseparable—does not in a significant sense *exist* apart—from the environment with which it interacts, the interaction being the foundation of consciousness.

Edelman observes, moreover, that for conscious animals, as is discernible in their early behavioral encounters, the world does not appear divided into preestablished categories. This suggests that in adapting to an "unlabeled world," a world filled with novelties, the consciousness bearing brain will be most successful if it acts not by instruction, not by preprogramming, but by a process of selection, not from the top down but from the bottom up. For Edelman, the brain is not like a computer because it is like a species. The neurons and repertoires made up of neurons are populations; they survive and flourish because through the variations within the populations they can continuously adapt themselves (which means changing the nature of the populations) as the organism moves through an ever-transforming and novelty-filled environment. For Edelman, consciousness is not computing; consciousness is selective adapting and readapting of itself to the demands of its shifting relationships with its unstable environment.

This view makes the survival value of consciousness conspicuous. If the brain functions thus selectively, it frees "animal behavior from the tyranny of ongoing events." Without consciousness, an animal will be at the mercy of "simultaneous but disparate environmental happenings." The organism without consciousness can do little more than "compute" input from the environment and adhere to preprogrammed responsive procedures. Consciousness enables an animal to meet very individual needs by regulating the salience of various elements of the vast stimulus complex that is the unstable environment it is perpetually encountering, both modifying the environment and being modified by it in the process of encounter.

Edelman is committed to the Darwinian insistence on the connection between man and the rest of the natural world. Human consciousness is different from that discernible in other creatures but not disconnected from their capacities. Edelman's findings, for example, regularly connect what he calls "higher consciousness," the consciousness that is found with certainty only in human beings and perhaps in chimpanzees, with what he calls "primary consciousness," which is found in many animals. He tries to explain how the nature of primary consciousness makes possible the development of "higher consciousness," what I am going to call "self-consciousness." That is, he tries to show how human beings in their most distinctive attribute derive from, are linked to, and are well fitted to a world of other natural creatures all following natural evolutionary processes.

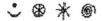

In order to understand the development of this natural, selective self-consciousness we must return to the cells and cell repertoires in the brain. The original development of the repertoires, of course, comes to an end with the conclusion of the embryonic processes (as do the developments of the lungs and other organs). Each brain repertoire of the newborn child has its own peculiar pattern of internal connections established by its unique history and situational context. Each repertoire, therefore, will respond differently from every other repertoire, even to the same stimulus. After birth the strength of the various repertoires' interconnections, furthermore, can and does change by means of molecular shifts caused by activities at synaptic junctions. These shifts permit the configuration of some repertoires in responding more strongly than others to enhance their linkages, to become more powerful parts of the brain system, whereas less successful repertoires will tend to atrophy, losing some of their "adherents" to their competitors.

A result of this competition is a further selection on top of the original embryological selection producing a continued development of multiple modes of response, just as the historical "accident" of a particular repertoire's original development allowed it to be "selected" by a stimulus entering the brain. There are in each newborn child's brain a number of differently arranged repertoires capable of responding in a similar but not identical fashion to the same stimulus. Processes of selection analogous to those that went into the embryological formation of the brain can function, then, as the basis of postnatal learning capacities of conscious organisms.

But to understand these capacities we must recognize how repertoires organize themselves. Neuronal repertoires aggregate into what Edelman calls maps. Neural maps are collections of cell repertoires linked to particular places in the brain, different kinds of maps existing in different portions of the brain, different maps created by the inflow from perceptions, and capable of undergoing modifications through the very processes of their activity. It is important to remember that these maps (unlike a physical geographer's) are like the repertoires in that they are continuously *self*-transforming, not fixed, even though they are topologically identifiable. Their power of development is especially significant because different maps may and normally do respond similarly but not identically to the same stimuli. Our perceptions normally are "entered," for example, not at just one place in the brain or through a single map. Our perceptions are taken into in our brain in a multiple fashion, through a variety of neuronal maps. This is one reason why much of the working of our brain must consist of sequential processes of selectivity. The maps, moreover, are continually communicating with one another. What they communicate includes not just reports of "outside" events but also stimulations and responses from "within" the maps themselves, these again providing material for selective decisions as to what is most salient to the individual organism at a given instant of its existence.

The adaptive value of this arrangement is particularly vivid if, like Edelman, one keeps in mind that brains exist in animals actively engaged in ever-changing, unpredictable environments. Precisely what these multiple, intercommunicating neuronal maps are good at is dealing with shifting and novel circumstances, determining the immediate saliency of what they encounter to the needs of a unique organism at this place and at this time. The saliency of a particular environmental event is established by the selections arrived at through the intercommunications among maps. What the maps accomplish through these intercommunicative processes is, first, to categorize perceptions, and then to recategorize them.

Learning cannot occur without a foundation of perceptual categorizings. These categorizings are conducted by primary consciousness. On the basis of internal criteria categories are determined according to salience of particular patterns among multiple maps, patterns resulting from the animal moving into, sampling, its changing environment. The crux of this process, let me repeat, is that perceptions "enter" the brain through not just one but a variety of maps. The intercommunications between the maps produce categorizations of the perceptions that are the foundation of primary consciousness.

The key process in this dynamic play of "topobiological" activities by which brain functions are continuously regulated or altered is what Edelman calls "re-entrant connectivities." These combine and recombine in a variety of ways the signals passing between maps. The exchange may be aroused by perceptions of the outside world picked up by different maps. The perceptions (even the same perceptions) are received differently, because the maps are differently constituted and located. So different parts of the brain signal back and forth to one another what each makes

of its "version" of the perceptions. This exchange, of course, may concern not external perceptions but "internal" activity within the brain maps themselves. In either case, each particular map's "versions" are continuously being "revised" or reentered by other maps.

Let us say that maps *a*, *b*, and *c* simultaneously receive perception *p*, which in fact is thus received as *p/a*, *p/b*, and *p/c*, since each map receives input according to its individual place and patterning. But *a* is immediately told by *b* and *c* about what they have received (just as *a* signals them of its reception), so *a* adjusts its original *p/a* to take account of *p/b* and *p/c*. The total process initiated is therefore one of categorization permitting, even encouraging, recategorization, since perceptions and organizings of perceptions can be continuously reentered into the process of intercommunicative activity in a variety of ways, continuously, phasically, recursively, and so forth.

My illustration is so oversimplified as to be dangerously distorting, but I hope it makes it plain that reentry is a selectively constructive function, not merely a corrective or a responsive one. Reentry differs radically, therefore, from feedback, which uses previous information in a fixed path for control and correction. Reentry occurs in selective systems in which the information, or kind of information, is not prespecified. Nor is the result prespecified, although it is likely to involve a strengthening of certain systems of connectivity. That strengthening, of course, will have influence on the next reentrant event. Reentry, most simply, is an essential process for making it possible for the brain to *recategorize*, to categorize its own unique categorizations. The power to recategorize is the ability to reorganize "old" systems in new ways to accommodate novel perceptions (either external or internal) or to make use of earlier perceptions in new fashions.

Memory, in Edelman's view, is fundamentally the ability to recategorize. Memory is not replicative and is not mediated by codes. Because it is, therefore, inexact, generalizing, and associative (because self-transforming), memory enables the brain to recognize, for example, various classes of things (often not much alike) under extremely diverse conditions. Memory is the ability—whose fullest power is realized only by animals capable of self-consciousness—to enhance the fundamental categorizing power of the brain "on the basis of past behavior and current context." Memory achieves this improvement of basic brain processes by bringing together previous perceptual categorizations with current perceptual input so that the individual organism is capable of judging the peculiar salience of present input to its past adaptations. It thereby establishes a basis for fitting the new element into past patterns or, contrarily, for shifting past patterns to accommodate the new element—or, most commonly I suspect, a little of both. In any event, the basis thus established becomes the ground for future recombinations.

Memory not as the repetition of fixed images but as a continuously operative recategorizing power or skill is the foundation, then, of learning capability. Learning capability is fundamentally the enhancing of the efficacy of various patterns of connections between brain maps. The "recurrence" of a specific perceptual categorization, for example, must be later in time than the original perceptual categorization. The later event therefore takes place in a different context, which requires a different but associated interaction between maps. This built-in "inexactness" of the remembering process is what makes remembering a skill rather than an automatic response. As a skill capable of improvement (strengthening, intensifying), memory makes feasible continuing, open-ended, self-transforming processes of further recategorizing. Memory enables learning processes that both develop and sustain self-consciousness to function in a self-enhancing fashion.

Self-consciousness, then, may be conceived of as the capacity of a unique "self-organizing" brain to deal selectively with an unstable environment full of novelties. It is the product of an individual history of a particular organism's development and its unique experiences after the completion of embryonic maturation. So although all human beings possess self-consciousness, nothing more distinguishes one human being from another than the peculiar character of each one's self-consciousness.

This is why Edelman identifies the crucial difference between primary consciousness and what I call self-consciousness as the emergence in an organism's brain of the power of distinguishing between self and nonself. The capacity to be conscious of being conscious permits the all-important discrimination between the existence of a self as a biological individual and the existence of a subjective individuality, the latter forming the basis for sociocultural systems. I will not here follow out his description of these phenomena, which culminate in the emergence of language. To do so would require discussion of very complex matters (including the

physical evolution of the vocal tract, the supralaryngeal space, and of Broca's and Wernicke's areas in hominids, because these permitted the development of language as a new system of *symbolic* recategorization). For my purposes, Edelman's description of the primary processes of brain development and function are most important because they create a credible picture of how our mental actions originate in and remain bound to well-understood physical characteristics of natural life processes.

Some of the persuasiveness of Edelman's representation lies in its explanation of humans' postnatal learning capabilities as taking shape in a fashion different from the processes of brain development from conception to birth yet still significantly analogous to, or derivative from, those processes. Both prenatal development and experiential learning employ the same basic systems of selection and adaptation. Edelman's explanations of the neural basis of learning suggest that it might be regarded as a continuation on a new plane, or reorientation into a new directionality, of processes that had operated in the organism from its earliest beginnings. These processes, moreover, are seen as functioning in accord with the principles by which macrobiological evolution takes place on a global basis.

An especially attractive feature of Neural Darwinism is that it conceives of mental life as "alive" in the same way that all other vital entities of which we have knowledge are "alive." Without diminishing the "purely" human attainment of self-consciousness and what self-consciousness can accomplish (of which his own work is a splendid example), Edelman thus represents human consciousness as totally "natural" but not at all mechanical. In his view, self-consciousness unequivocally is an appropriate development of less intricately organized life forms, because it is a wonderful adaptation to the mutable conditions of our planet.[3]

Indeed, so far as Edelman is correct, we are better adapted to natural existence on this globe than any other species. Nothing beats self-consciousness for dealing with the ever-changing environments featured by our earth. Self-consciousness even enables us, unlike other species that develop self-destructively, to control the self-destructive impetus of our biological success. If Edelman is right, humankind is not alienated by its attainment of self-consciousness. To the contrary, self-consciousness proves that if there is any one species that especially *belongs* in the earth's biosphere it is *homo sapiens*. Wordsworth was right: we are superbly fitted to nature and nature is fitted to our development, even, as Wordsworth dared to suggest, to underwriting the evolution of culture.

Yet the primary threat to mankind now (as if we were playing out a script by a Greek tragedian) is surely our explosive success as a species. Our destruction seems most likely to come from ourselves. We have developed to the point where we can annihilate ourselves by destroying the environment that has encouraged our amazing success. Ecological awareness is essential to preventing the insanity of such suicide, whether through weaponry, pollution, or sheer overpopulation.

The great test of our times is whether or not we are willing to undertake the responsibilities, and accept the sacrifices, that are now incumbent upon human societies if we are not foolishly to degrade the special beneficence of our environment to ourselves. The ecological thinking upon which responsible behavior must be based, however, should consist of something more than scientific studies. It requires as well the shaping of emotional attitudes, the strengthening of particular kinds of imagining, and the accepting of certain ethical commitments.[4] To these tasks an ecological literary criticism can contribute more than a little; and a useful way to begin, as I have attempted to demonstrate, is to understand the significance of the proto-ecological character of romantic poetry.

Shelley's definitions of both the nature and the function of imagining, for instance, are given a surprising degree of validation by the theory of Neural Darwinism, which supports as well the significance of Wordsworth's efforts to develop a new understanding of memory as a creative rather than a mechanistic process. Edelman's findings renew the interest and even relevance of romantic attempts to arrive at what I have called a biological understanding of mind and what he calls a "biologically based epistemology." It is not, however, so much the romantics'"success" as anticipators of evolutionary and ecological thinking that makes a reassessment of their purposes and practices so rewarding as it is the recognition compelled by such revaluations of how dangerously constrictive and socially threatening the currently dominant modes of literary criticism have become. By reconstructing the conceptual patterns through which romanticism has come to be understood we may open the way to reconceiving the functions of literary art in advanced technological societies.

Misreadings of romantic poetry, then, are not a trivial matter. As I have pointed out, they reflect underlying presuppositions in contemporary

criticism that cripple humanistic studies from addressing possible solutions of practical social problems afflicting our desperately overcrowded world. Among these assumptions I have singled out that which effectively segregates human beings and human cultures from all other natural phenomena. As dangerous as this inverse transcendentalism, however, is the popular pseudohistoricism that reduces the intricate play of contingent human and natural events to schematized oppositional power struggles. At the root of these attitudes is a resistance to—oftentimes amounting to a hatred of—individuality and uniqueness in people, peoples, and their cultural accomplishments. Romantic poetry is important today because it is the last major artistic expression of an overriding belief in the practical social preciousness of unique acts of imagination. It is that belief, which results in a conception of the supreme value of the individuality of interdependence, to which Neural Darwinism offers scientific validation. A better understanding of romanticism might become, therefore, a small but solid base for a radical reassessment of the intellectual character and educational functions of present-day literary criticism.

I do not pretend to prophetic insight as to where the rethinking I propose may lead. It seems reasonable to suspect, however, that it might produce a more cosmopolitan understanding of the value of the diversity of cultures, and the diversity of the products of those cultures. It might, that is to say, free so-called multicultural discourse from its current defensiveness and negativism, the tendency to define a people, a nation, or an ethnic group only in opposition to others, seeking escape from oppression only by oppressing or denigrating others, ignoring the possibilities for creative progress through recognition of mutual interdependencies. It might, at the least, begin a helpful reorientation of current critical thinking toward more concern for practical ethical responsibility among those advantaged by their advanced education.

Putting aside predictions, however, we should, I believe, confront unhesitatingly the fact that the evidence of biological studies such as Edelman's tells heavily against the underpinnings of the ideological commitments of most currently prominent literary critics. These, with the notable exception of some feminists, have committed themselves to ideological positions that either in effect dismiss the worth of detailed and sophisticated knowledge of natural processes as irrelevant to cultural studies, or make use of static, schematized, and obsolete scientific conceptions of "nature" as a basis for their critical pronouncements. None to date has considered the scientific evidence presented by researchers such as Edelman that humankind is almost uniquely fitted to this planet, and that cultural studies might best begin by thinking first about the relation of humankind to the continuing evolution of life on earth. This is our home, but not ours alone, where we dwell not as isolates but as participants (responsible participants, one hopes) in a remarkably dynamic interplay of thousands of millions of diverse vitalities. From the perspective of our time, therefore, it seems worthwhile to recognize that Wordsworth was prophetic in his articulation of an essential romantic creed. Great imaginations can and should speak of the simple produce of the common day and of nothing more than what we are, because nothing more astonishing has been produced on this earth than the myriad individualities of being that we encompass in the term *humankind*. Wonderful and challenging still is Wordsworth's belief that the yet lovely earth is our true and proper home, where in the end we find our happiness, or not at all.

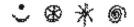

notes

1. Introducing Ecological Criticism

1. Jonathan Bate, *Romantic Ecology* (London: Routledge, 1991), 16–17.

2. Alan Bewell, *William Wordsworth and the Age of Enlightenment* (New Haven: Yale University Press, 1989).

3. Tilottima Rajan, *The Supplement of Reading: Figures of Understanding in Romantic Theory and Practice* (Ithaca: Cornell University Press, 1990).

4. Paul Magnuson, "The Politics of 'Frost at Midnight,'" *Wordsworth Circle* 22 (1991): 3–11.

5. Tobin Siebers, in *Cold War Criticism and the Politics of Skepticism*, an early sketch of which appeared as "Cold War Criticism," *Common Knowledge* 1, no. 3 (1992): 60–90, analyzes in scrupulous detail the effects upon criticism of shifts in the history of U.S.-Soviet relations after World War II. Although I hesitate to insist on such direct parallels, I recognize the aptness of Siebers's description of the mentality fostered in Cold War criticism as one that "overestimates our tendency to miscalculate, and . . . thinks the worst of other people's interpretations and intentions . . . is suspicious of emotions, claims for morality, altruism" (63). Siebers's perspective enables him to provide an illuminating context for social phenomena, such as "the radical sixties," for which most historians of criticism have been unable to establish coherent relationships to preceding and subsequent developments.

6. Marjorie Levinson, "The Immortality Ode," in *Wordsworth's Great Period Poems* (Cambridge: Cambridge University Press, 1986); Paul de Man, "Shelley Disfigured," in *The Rhetoric of Romanticism* (New York: Columbia University Press, 1984).

7. I follow the text of the poem (first published in *Murray's Magazine* 1 (1887): 145–46) of Leslie Marchand, *Byron: A Portrait* Chicago: University of Chicago Press,

1970), 450–51. E. H. Coleridge gave the verses the title by which they are usually known, "Love and Death."

8. In my book *British Romantic Art* (Berkeley and Los Angeles: University of California Press, 1986) I have explored in depth reasons underlying the centrality of the romantic insistence on pleasure as the source and goal of art, pointing out that Freud's grim distinction between "the pleasure principle" and "the reality principle" has obscured the romantics' contrary belief in our need to subsume the latter principle in the former, to recognize that the real is intrinsically pleasurable: see 230, and the lengthy n. 22 on 249.

9. *Proto-ecological* unfortunately may suggest that the romantics were trying to be ecological but could not make it, which would be silly. The term may even suggest that I believe the romantics would have been better poets had they had our knowledge, which would be equally absurd. *Proto-ecological*, finally, may carry the connotation that biological science, like its sister disciplines, has moved in simple, linear, progressive fashion from childish fantasies into the mature wisdom of today. Many scientists, in fact, believe that, but I do not. Science, like all cultural enterprises, "develops" in weirdly complicated, even contradictory, fashions, and what we think of as certain truth in a century will probably seem childishly fantastic and ill-informed. Still, I have not found a better term than *proto-ecological* to summarize the directionality of the romantics' thinking about nature, and their working, occasionally very much to their advantage, along evolutionary lines that had not yet crystallized into the Darwinian patterns that for the past 130 years have focused biological debates.

10. Jessica Benjamin, *The Bonds of Love* (New York: Methuen, 1988), 184.

11. Ibid., 185. Benjamin draws heavily on works such as Evelyn Keller's *Reflections on Gender and Science* (New Haven: Yale University Press, 1985).

12. In chap. 6 of my *Romantic Fantasy and Science Fiction* (New Haven: Yale University Press, 1988), 95–116, I have analyzed the emergence of the feminine within the poet in the "Ode to Psyche."

13. Quoted by Benjamin, 192.

14. Carol Gilligan's *In a Different Voice* (Cambridge, Mass.: Harvard University Press, 1982) may be cited as another excellent feminist analysis, in this case of moral psychology, whose critiques and conclusions seem very much in accord with ecological conceptions.

15. It seems to me far from coincidental that in the late eighteenth century women made real contributions to the development of scientific obstetrics, botany, and biology—the only disciplines in which they could then participate.

16. My citation is from *The Poetical Works of William Wordsworth*, 2d ed., 5 vols., ed. Ernest de Selincourt and Helen Darbishire (Oxford: Clarendon, 1954), vol. 4, 110. The poem was composed in May 1802 and first published in the *Morning Post* on 6 September 1802, the topical reference being the celebration of Buonaparte's birthday on which he was confirmed consul for life. My reading of this sonnet is indebted to Christina Root's Columbia University dissertation on Napoleon and the English Romantic poets.

1. introducing ecological criticism

17. "Normal" or "natural," of course, to most of Wordsworth's audience. Present-day readers, especially feminists, may with justice object that Wordsworth's representation follows traditional arbitrary conceptions of gender. The validity of such criticism, however, ought not to obscure the radicalness of the poet's deflation of Buonaparte by an appeal to "natural" domesticities.

18. The self-deceptions of revolutionary thought are brilliantly analyzed by Fyodor Dostoyevsky, perhaps most revealingly through the character of Shigalov, who beginning with the idea of unlimited freedom finds himself inexorably espousing unlimited despotism. See *The Devils*, trans. David Magarshak (1971; reprint, London: Penguin, 1987), 404.

19. *The Poems of Samuel Taylor Coleridge*, ed. E. H. Coleridge (1912; reprint, London: Oxford University Press, 1960), 243. All my citations of Coleridge's poetry are taken from this edition.

20. "Population thinking" as used by biologists today in a more technical sense derives from Darwin's insistence on the importance of variation within a population as producing diverse classes of organisms by gradual selective processes, a mode of thinking that, as Gerald M. Edelman points out in *Bright Air, Brilliant Fire: On the Matter of the Mind* (New York: Basic Books, 1992), 73, contrasts starkly with Platonic essentialism and is unknown in physics.

21. J. J. Spengler, *French Predecessors of Malthus* (Durham, N.C.: Duke University Press, 1942), describes earlier students of population. Kenneth Smith, *The Malthusian Controversy* (London: Longmans, 1951), is still useful on the history of the battles over Malthus's proposals.

22. *Shelley: Poetical Works*, new ed., ed. Thomas Hutchinson and corrected by G. M. Matthews (London: Oxford University Press, 1970), 812. A little earlier in the same poem Shelley speaks of "A Spirit of activity and life" diffused throughout the universe "That knows no term, cessation, or decay" (6.786.148–49), which accurately epitomizes his romantic a-religious Spinozism.

23. It is surprising that despite Alfred North Whitehead's praise of Shelley's scientific capabilities in 1925, and the follow-up on his suggestions many years ago by Carl Grabo and Desmond King-Hele, there is still no book on Shelley's scientific knowledge equivalent to Hermione de Almeida's recent splendid study of Keats, to which I refer subsequently, or to Trevor H. Levere's indispensable study of Coleridge's scientific knowledge, *Poetry Realized in Nature* (Cambridge: Cambridge University Press, 1981), which is ably supplemented by Raimonda Modiano, *Coleridge and the Concept of Nature* (Tallahassee: Florida State University Press, 1985). Wordsworth's relation to the intellectual currents of his day has been even better served in a variety of works, several of which are cited in later chapters.

24. Charles W. Hagelman, Jr., "Keats's Medical Training and the Last Stanza of the 'Ode to Psyche,' " *Keats-Shelley Journal* 3 (1962): 73–82. Hagelman's observation is elab-

orated on by Donald C. Goellnicht, *The Poet-Physician: Keats and Medical Science* (Pittsburgh: University of Pittsburgh Press, 1984), 135–39, with sensitive perceptiveness.

25. John Aikin, *An Essay on the Application of Natural History to Poetry* (1777; reprint, New York: Garland, 1970), 2–10. On the very important change from "natural philosophy" to "natural history" see Carl Woodring, *Nature into Art* (Cambridge, Mass.: Harvard University Press, 1989), 38.

26. Preface to *Lyrical Ballads*, cited from *The Prose Works of William Wordsworth*, 3 vols., ed. W.J.B. Owen and Jane Worthington Smyser (Oxford: Clarendon, 1974), vol. 1, 141.

27. Alan Liu, *Wordsworth: The Sense of History* (Stanford: Stanford University Press, 1989), thus epitomizes the new historicist negation of nature on p. 38, explaining on the following page that there is no nature because "what there 'is' is history." It is revealing that Liu, along with Marjorie Levinson and Jerome McGann, though emphasizing a commitment to Marxist ideology, so consistently disregards the relevant criticism of Raymond Williams. In *The Country and the City* (New York: Oxford University Press, 1973), for example, Williams addresses many issues central to the evolution of ecological thinking: see for example chap. 13, "The Green Language," which explores the emergence of a "new consciousness" of the natural world that produced a new "confidence in nature, in its own workings, which . . . was also a broader, more humane confidence in men" (127).

2. Feminism and the Historicity of Science

1. This translation of W. C. Allen is described as excellent by the most careful student of this phase of Haeckel's career, Robert C. Stauffer, "Haeckel, Darwin, and Ecology," *Quarterly Review of Biology* 32 (1957): 138–44, 143.

2. Stauffer's essay, cited in the preceding note, demonstrates that Haeckel's principal aim in the work in which he coined the term *ecology* was to familiarize the German scientific community with Darwin's ideas, his bias suggested by the title of his book, *Morphologie der Organismen: Allgemenine Grundzüge der organischen Formen-Wissenschaft, mechanisch begründet durch die von Charles Darwin reformirte Descendenz-Theorie.*

3. Annotators of the French translation of the *Asiatic Researches*, in which Jones's work appeared, included Lamarck and Cuvier. Ernest Mayr, *The Growth of Biological Thought* (Cambridge, Mass.: Harvard University Press, 1982), is one of the important historians of science to point out how difficult it was for the concept of extinction to be accepted even as late as the eighteenth century (thus its importance in Byron's *Cain* as discussed here in chap. 7). Mayr notes that extinction was as objectionable to Newtonians as it was to natural theologians, because it appeared to vitiate "natural laws" (347–48). Analyses such as Mayr's focus attention on a radicalism in Darwin's theory often overlooked by nonbiologists—namely, that it gives a preeminent role to chance.

4. Jack Major, "Historical Development of the Ecosystem Concept," *The Ecosystem Concept in Natural Resource Management*, ed. George M. Van Dyne (London: Academic

2. feminism and the historicity of science

Press, 1969), 9–21. A valuable introduction for nonspecialists to the eighteenth-century scientific developments from which the romantics worked is *The Ferment of Knowledge*, ed. G. S. Rousseau and Roy Porter (Cambridge: Cambridge University Press, 1980). Especially illuminating is Jacques Roger's essay "The Living World," 255–84, which lucidly traces, for instance, how and when mechanistic conceptions of life processes gave way to vitalistic ones (eighteenth-century vitalism, of course, being quite different from its late nineteenth-century namesake) and the reasons why Cuvier's paleontological research led him away from Lamarck's evolutionary thinking; Roy Porter's "The Terraqueous Globe," 285–326; and Maurice Crosland's "Chemistry and the Chemical Revolution," 389–416, which demonstrates how shrewd T. S. Kuhn was in his *Structure of Scientific Revolutions*, rev. ed. (Chicago: University of Chicago Press, 1970), to seize on Lavoisier's "chemical revolution" as a prime example of his paradigm-shift theory. Extensive annotations in all these essays make them unusually useful to the nonspecialist.

5. Published by Cambridge University Press in 1985.

6. Donald Worster, *Nature's Economy: The Roots of Ecology* (San Francisco: Harper, 1977).

7. Clarence Glacken, *Traces from the Rhodian Shore: Nature and Culture in Western Thought from Ancient Times to the End of the Eighteenth Century* (Berkeley and Los Angeles: University of California Press, 1967).

8. Robert McIntosh, "Ecosystems, Evolution, and Relationship Patterns of Living Organisms," *American Scientist* 52 (1963): 246–67, 249.

9. Karl Kroeber, *Romantic Fantasy and Science Fiction* (New Haven: Yale University Press, 1988), 14–20.

10. "The knowledge both of the Poet and the Man of science is pleasure; but the knowledge of the one cleaves to us as a necessary part of our existence, our natural and unalienable inheritance; the other is a personal and individual acquisition, slow to come to us, and by no habitual and direct sympathy connecting us with our fellow-beings. The Man of science seeks truth as a remote and unknown benefactor; he cherishes and loves it in his solitude; the Poet, singing a song in which all human beings join with him, rejoices in the presence of truth as our visible friend and hourly companion." *The Prose Works of William Wordsworth*, 3 vols., ed. W.J.B. Owen and Jane Worthington Smyser (Oxford: Clarendon, 1974). Preface to "Lyrical Ballads" (1850), vol. 1, 141.

11. Richard Feynman, *QED: The Strange Theory of Light and Matter* (Princeton: Princeton University Press, 1985). This splendid book, which probably comes as close as is possible to explaining quantum electrodynamics to blockheads like me, originated in lectures, and Feynman carries over his oral introduction to his third lecture to begin his third chapter: "Some of you haven't heard the other two lectures and will find this lecture almost incomprehensible. Those of you who *have* heard the other two lectures will also find this lecture incomprehensible, but you know that's all right: as I explained in the first lecture, the way we have to describe Nature is generally incomprehensible to us" (77).

12. Anna Bramwell, *Ecology in the Twentieth Century: A History* (New Haven: Yale University Press, 1989), 205. A major portion of Bramwell's excellent book is concerned with the Nazis and ecology.

13. Evelyn Keller, *Reflections on Gender and Science* (New Haven: Yale University Press, 1985), 170. Keller quotes Monod's remark on 167.

14. Quoted by Keller, ibid., 165.

15. Published by Columbia University Press in 1980.

16. E. M. Forster, *Howards End* (New York: Knopf, 1921), 261.

3. Surprised by Nature: Ecology and Cold War Criticism

1. Jonathan Bate, *Romantic Ecology* (London: Routledge, 1991), 4.

2. Paul de Man, "Intentional Structure of the Romantic Image," *The Rhetoric of Romanticism* (New York: Columbia University Press, 1984), 16; Geoffrey Hartman, *Wordsworth's Poetry, 1787–1814* (1964; reprint, Cambridge, Mass.: Harvard University Press, 1987), 293–94.

3. Jerome J. McGann, *The Romantic Ideology: A Critical Investigation* (Chicago: University of Chicago Press, 1983).

4. Marjorie Levinson's essay on the "Immortality Ode" appears in her *Wordsworth's Great Period Poems* (Cambridge: Cambridge University Press, 1986); while Alan Liu's summary assertion appears in his *Wordsworth: The Sense of History* (Stanford: Stanford University Press, 1989), 38.

5. Wordsworth's first visit in 1793 was probably in late July or early August, when, after separating from Raisely Calvert near Salisbury, he traveled alone, mostly on foot, to the home of his friend Robert Jones in North Wales. The power of critical convention appears vividly in the repeated emphasis of recent commentaries on the possible relation of "Tintern Abbey" to the fall of the Bastille nine years before, at the cost of ignoring the "similitude-within-dissimilitude" of Wordsworth's two visits to the same locale so insisted upon in the poem's opening: "Five years have past; five summers, with the length / Of five long winters!"

6. *Basic Writings of Nietzsche*, trans. and ed. Walter Kaufman (New York: Random House, 1968), 393.

7. Alan Bewell, *William Wordsworth and the Age of Enlightenment* (New Haven: Yale University Press, 1989), focuses, of course, on Wordsworth's indebtedness to the emergence of environmental historicism in the eighteenth century and his development of a new kind of "anthropological" vision; Larry J. Swingle, *The Obstinate Questionings of English Romanticism* (Baton Rouge: Louisiana State University Press, 1987), especially in chap. 1, " The Romantic Situation," provides an elegantly comprehensive survey of the intellectual and aesthetic circumstances giving rise to romanticism in England; in her chapter "Romanticism in England," in *Romanticism in National Context*, ed. Roy Porter

and Mikulas Teich (Cambridge: Cambridge University Press, 1988), Marilyn Butler persuasively argues that English romanticism's origin "has to be dated from about 1740" (39), because this expansive cultural revolution drew upon such phenomena as the growth of a new reading public, the "country movement," and the burgeoning of serious studies of popular language.

8. Nathan Rosenberg and L. E. Birdzell, Jr., *How the West Grew Rich: The Economic Transformation of the Industrial World* (New York: Basic Books, 1986), especially chap. 5, "The Development of Industry: 1750–1880," 144–88, are lucidly effective at demonstrating the relationships among diverse segments of economic, technological, and social developments.

9. "Lines" is cited from the 1798 text in *Lyrical Ballads*, rev. ed., ed. R. L. Brett and A. R. Jones (1963; reprint, London: Methuen, 1965), 69. Unless otherwise indicated all citations from *Lyrical Ballads* are to this edition.

10. Wordsworth's observation appeared in the "advertisement" to the 1798 *Lyrical Ballads*, *The Prose Works of William Wordsworth*, 3 vols., ed. W.J.B. Owen and Jane W. Smyser (Oxford: Clarendon, 1974), vol. 1, 115. Shelley's phrase, of course, is from "Mont Blanc."

11. Brett and Jones, 154.

12. *Byron: Poetical Works*, new ed., ed. Frederick Page, corrected by John Jump (Oxford: Oxford University Press, 1986), 366.

13. This last citation is from *The Ruined Cottage* and *The Pedlar*, ed. James Butler (Ithaca: Cornell University Press, 1979), ms. D, 75. The preceding (like the following) is from *William Wordsworth: Selected Poems and Prefaces*, ed. Jack Stillinger (Boston: Houghton-Mifflin, 1965), 43–44.

14. The first extended study of Shelley's indebtedness to Wordsworth is G. Kim Blank's excellent *Wordsworth's Influence on Shelley* (New York: St. Martins, 1988). I read Shelley's famous sonnet "To Wordsworth," published with *Alastor* in 1816, as expressive, as the young poet says, of genuine grief that the "Poet of Nature" has abandoned his "rock-built refuge."

4. Poetic Ecosystems: Art for Nature's Sake

1. Karl Kroeber, " 'Home at Grasmere': Ecological Holiness," *PMLA* 89 (1974): 132–41.

2. Kenneth Johnston, *Wordsworth and the Recluse* (New Haven: Yale University Press, 1984); David Simpson, *Wordsworth and the Historical Imagination* (London: Methuen, 1987); and Thomas McFarland, *William Wordsworth: Industry and Achievement* (Oxford: Clarendon, 1992), all offer perceptive and illuminating praise of the accomplishments of "Home at Grasmere."

3. All my citations are from ms. B as reproduced in *Home at Grasmere*, ed. Beth Darlington (Ithaca: Cornell University Press, 1977). The opening of the poem, in which the

poet says, "I forgot / My haste, for hasty had my footsteps been" (6–7), is evidence that Wordsworth is exploiting to the full the origins of the word *dwell*, which are to be associated with straying from a track. The research of Toby Benis in her Columbia University dissertation documents the consistency of this paradoxical union of "home" and "vagrancy" in Wordsworth's early poetry. A major element in the interrelating of dwelling with wandering is Wordsworth's identification of peace and movement, or in the words of "Home at Grasmere," "rest" and "motion." As a meditation on "dwelling" the poem richly rewards comparison with Martin Heidegger's "Building Dwelling Thinking," available in *Poetry, Language, Thought*, trans. Albert Hofstadter (New York: Harper and Row, 1971), 145–61. The Wordsworthian ideas of "rest" and "motion" also seem to me closely linked to the romantic "punctuated equilibrium" concepts of evolution.

4. Alan Bewell, *William Wordsworth and the Age of Enlightenment* (New Haven: Yale University Press, 1989), 39–41.

5. Thomas McFarland, *Coleridge and the Pantheist Tradition* (Oxford: Clarendon, 1969), especially "The Spinozistic Crescendo," 53–106.

6. Yirmiyahu Yovel, *Spinoza and Other Heretics* (Princeton: Princeton University Press, 1989), ix.

7. Stuart Hampshire,*Spinoza* (Harmondsworth: Penguin, 1951), 47.

8. Jacques Monod, *Chance and Necessity*, trans. Austyn Wainhouse (London: Collins, 1972), 13.

9. This perception is the foundation of Edelman's analyses of the biological foundations of consciousness: see chap. 9.

10. Quotations from "Nutting" are from the Brett-Jones edition of *Lyrical Ballads* (1963; reprint, London: Methuen, 1965), 196–98. The commentary on "Nutting" is enormous, in part because of textual intricacies and dramatic changes in various drafts of the poem (which at one time was included in *The Prelude*)—a good introduction to these intricacies being the commentary of Hugh Sykes Davies in *Wordsworth and the Worth of Words*, ed. John Kenig and Jonathan Wordsworth (Cambridge: Cambridge University Press, 1986), 264–70. Among the notable psychological readings one might cite, if only for their diversity, those of Geoffrey Hartman in his *Wordsworth's Poetry, 1787–1814* (Cambridge, Mass.: Harvard University Press, 1964); Margaret Homans, *Women Writers and Poetic Identity* (Princeton: Princeton University Press, 1980); and Jonathan Arac, *Critical Genealogies: Historical Situations for Postmodern Literary Studies* (New York: Columbia University Press, 1987). Rachel Crawford, "The Structure of the Sororal in Wordsworth's 'Nutting,' " *Studies in Romanticism* 31, no. 2 (1992): 197–212, makes excellent use of her predecessors' work to develop an interesting shift away from focus upon maternal psychology in the poem.

11. A noteworthy exception is the effort of Clifford H. Siskin, *The Historicity of Romantic Discourse* (New York: Oxford University Press, 1988), to understand what their emerging profession meant to the romantic poets; and in several essays Karen Swann has

sensitively probed the same issue from a different perspective—see, for instance, "Harassing the Muse," in *Romanticism and Feminism*, ed. Anne K. Mellor (Bloomington: University of Indiana Press, 1988).

5. Discovering Nature's Voice

1. Geoffrey H. Hartman, "Wordsworth, Inscriptions, and Romantic Nature Poetry," in *From Sensibility to Romanticism*, ed. Frederick W. Hilles and Harold Bloom (New York: Oxford University Press, 1965), 389–413; this extremely valuable essay, to which my thinking about Wordsworth's lyricism is much indebted, was later reprinted in Hartman's collection *Beyond Formalism: Literary Essays, 1958–1970* (New Haven: Yale University Press, 1970).

2. *Lyrical Ballads*, rev. ed., ed. R. L. Brett and A. R. Jones (London: Methuen, 1965), 38. All citations from *Lyrical Ballads* in this chapter are to this edition, which reproduces texts from the 1798 edition.

3. "To the Nightingale," in *The Poems of Samuel Taylor Coleridge*, ed. E. H. Coleridge (1912; reprint, London: Oxford University Press, 1960), 93–94.

4. By far the best commentary on "The Nightingale" is that of Fred V. Randel, "Coleridge and the Contentiousness of Romantic Nightingales," *Studies in Romanticism* 21, no. 1 (1982): 33–56, to which my criticism is indebted. Susan Luther, in " 'A Different Lore': Coleridge's 'The Nightingale,' " *Wordsworth Circle* 20, no. 2 (1989): 91–97, reads the poem's opening negatives quite differently from the way I do; whereas Gene M. Bernstein, "The Recreating Secondary Imagination in Coleridge's 'The Nightingale,' " *ELH* 48 (1981): 341–42, sees the negatives as part of Coleridge's "task of deconstruction."

5. In his letter to Wordsworth containing "The Nightingale" Coleridge included a humorous series of couplets asking, "like an honest bard, dear Wordsworth, / You'll tell me what you think my Bird's worth." After suggesting the bird's music is not too bad, Coleridge concludes, "Yet, sure; no wonder it should breed, / That my bird's tail's a tail indeed / And makes its own inglorious harmony / Aeolio crepitu, non carmine." See *Lyrical Ballads*, ed. Michael Mason (London: Longmans, 1992), 33–34, for full text and a commentary.

Disregard for Coleridge's discomfort with Wordsworth's ideas and attitudes leading to misstatements about and misinterpretations of both his friend's poetry and his critical prose (one of the most crippling misprisions of Cold War romantic criticism) seems finally beginning to be rectified: see, for example, the valuable essay by Thomas Pfau, " 'Elementary Feelings' and 'Distorted Language': The Pragmatics of Culture in Wordsworth's Preface to *Lyrical Ballads*," *New Literary History* 24 (1993): 125–46. A pioneering essay in this direction was Don H. Bialostosky's "Coleridge's Interpretation of Wordsworth's Preface to *Lyrical Ballads*," *PMLA* 93 (1978): 912–24.

6. Citations from Keats's poetry are all from *The Poems of John Keats*, ed. Jack Stillinger (Cambridge, Mass.: Harvard University Press, 1978). At Keats's one meeting with Coleridge the older poet spoke of (among a welter of other matters) nightingales: see *The*

Letters of John Keats, ed. Hyder E. Rollins, 2 vols. (Cambridge, Mass.: Harvard University Press, 1958), vol. 2, 88.

7. Beth Lau, *Keats's Reading of the Romantic Poets* (Ann Arbor: University of Michigan Press, 1991), provides a systematic compilation of verbal echoes of the earlier poets in Keats's verse. Such a compilation cannot, of course, capture the kind of nuance of response with which I am here concerned, though it can direct the critic to significant echo points.

8. "It struck me, what quality went to form a Man of Achievement especially in Literature & which Shakespeare possessed so enormously—I mean *Negative Capability*, that is when man is capable of being in uncertainties, Mysteries, doubts, without any irritable reaching after fact & reason—Coleridge, for instance, would let go by a fine isolated verisimilitude caught from the Penetralium of mystery, from being incapable of remaining content with half knowledge." Letter of 21–27 December 1817 to George and Tom Keats, *The Letters of John Keats*, ed. Hyder E. Rollins, 2 vols. (Cambridge, Mass.: Harvard University Press, 1958), vol. 1, 193–94.

An important essay by Mark Jones, "Double Economics: Ambivalence in Wordsworth's Pastoral," *PMLA* 108, no. 5 (October 1993): 1089–1113, describes the "evaluative crossovers" that made Wordsworth so liberating a poet for a contemporary like Keats who admired "negative capability." Jones, by showing how "Michael" dramatizes "the opposed symbologies on which pastoral turns" (1105), illuminates why the romantics brought together contrastive modes of valuing to elucidate the strengths and limitations of each. This preference for the complexity of "both-and" to the simplification of "either-or" judgments, although uncongenial to a Cold War mind-set, was almost a necessity for poets who conceived of the intersecting of incommensurate forces as a fundamental condition of human life. The core of Wordsworth's "betrayal" for his younger contemporaries lay in his reducing to a single standard the various "cross-valuations" characteristic of his early art, the change illustrated by his revising of *The Ruined Cottage* discussed in chap. 3.

A more generalized description of how romantic poems present diverse valuation systems interactively rather than oppositionally appears in Kurt Heinzelman, *The Economics of the Imagination* (Amherst: University of Massachusetts Press, 1980), esp. 4–20.

9. *The Poetical Works of William Wordsworth*, 2d ed., ed. Ernest de Selincourt, 5 vols. (Oxford: Clarendon, 1952), vol. 2, 206. Were this book anything more than an introduction to its subject, I would discuss *The Prelude*, one Focus being Wordsworth's recovery of moral health less from social than from natural agencies.

6. Malthusian Visions

1. John Maynard Keynes, *Essays in Biography* (New York: Knopf, 1933), 120.

2. *Shelley's Poetry and Prose*, ed. Donald H. Reiman and Sharon B. Powers (New York: Norton, 1977), 301–2.

6. malthusian visions

3. Ibid., 305. The French Revolution has of course been the focus of most of this century's studies of crowd and mob psychology, although new historicists have rather slighted this feature of history in their concern over subjective displacements. Georges Lefebvre's work in this field is seminal, including the crucial essay "Les Foules Revolutionnaires," *Les Annales Historiques de la Revolution Francaise* 11 (1934): 1–26; and such works as *The Great Fear*, trans. John White (New York: Random House, 1973). Also notable is the work of George Rudé, especially *The Crowd in History: A Study of Popular Disturbances in France and England 1730–1848* (New York: Wiley, 1964); and subsequently that of scholars like Robert A. Nye, *The Origins of Crowd Psychology* (London: Sage Publications, 1975). I have not yet found, however, any adequate discussion of Shelley's originality in conceiving of "the people" as capable of extraordinary moral power through their existence as a multitude.

4. In *British Romantic Art* (Berkeley and Los Angeles: University of California Press, 1985) I have discussed the romantic geographic or naturalistic patriotism (see especially 85–93), describing Coleridge's "Fears in Solitude" as paradigmatic for later poems such as Shelley's *Mask of Anarchy* that appeal to the land (meant literally, not figuratively) of England as the source of the English people's highest virtues.

5. *An Essay on the Principle of Population*, ed. Antony Flew (Harmondsworth: Penguin, 1970), 134. My citations of Malthus throughout are to this edition of Malthus's 1798 edition, which I use because it is relatively accessible and contains a useful introduction, even though the text is marred by some typographical errors.

6. It should be observed that although Malthus speaks only of subsistence, his perception of what is needed for the production of food—fertilizers, for example—endows his predictions with relevance to forms of exploitation and pollution more intensely developed after his lifetime.

7. In the brief appendix to this chapter I try to illuminate one aspect of Malthus's unpopularity, but it is worth observing the ironic fact that early birth-control devices were often referred to as Malthusian devices; see Peter Fryer, *The Birth Controllers* (London: Collins, 1965); and Margaret Sanger's still-moving *My Fight for Birth Control* (New York: Farrar and Rinehart, 1931).

8. Journal-letter to George and Georgiana Keats, from 14 February to 3 May 1819, entry of 21 April, in *The Letters of John Keats*, ed. Hyder E. Rollins, 2 vols. (Cambridge, Mass.: Harvard University Press, 1958), vol. 2, 102–3.

9. Hermione de Almeida, *Romantic Medicine and John Keats* (New York: Oxford University Press, 1991).

10. On environmental historicism see Alan Bewell's splendid book *Wordsworth and the Enlightenment* (New Haven: Yale University Press, 1989). Bewell rightly emphasizes the role of geology in romantic thought, even political thought, for this "historicizing of the earth" underlay evolutionary tendencies in various kinds of biological research and speculation.

11. Or so I dare correct what I take to be Keats's misspelling, which produces the splendid nonword *interassimulate*: "Men who live together have a silent moulding and influencing power over each other—They interassimulate." Letter to the George Keatses of 21 September 1819, *The Letters of John Keats*, vol. 2, 208.

For good summary judgments of Lamarck see Leslie Gaylord Simpson, *The Meaning of Evolution* (1949; reprint, New York: New American Library, 1959), 126–27; and Joseph Anthony Mazzeo, *The Design of Life* (New York: Pantheon, 1967), 106–11. Ernest Mayr, *The Growth of Biological Thought* (Cambridge, Mass.: Harvard University Press, 1982), gives extended attention to Lamarck and lucidly defines the various strengths of his thinking, research, and use of his predecessors. Mayr gets rid of the habit of dismissing Lamarck by knee-jerk references to "inheritance of acquired characteristics" by articulating Larmarck's emphasis on evolutionary change as caused in good measure by the capacity of genera, species, and individuals to react to special environmental conditions (353). Mayr's judicious appraisal is in keeping with recent tendencies among students of evolution to recognize the importance of romantic predecessors of Charles Darwin. Stephen Jay Gould, for instance, who in his chapter "Episodic Evolutionary Change" in *The Panda's Thumb* (New York: Norton, 1980) associates Lamarck with his description of evolutionary processes in terms of "punctuated equilibrium." Gould observes that "lineages change little during most of their history, but events of rapid speciation occasionally punctuate this tranquility. Evolution is the differential survival and deployment of these punctuations" (184).

12. "Epistle to John Hamilton Reynolds," lines 93–107, in *The Poems of John Keats*, ed. Jack Stillinger (Cambridge, Mass.: Harvard University Press, 1978), 244.

7. Refiguring Reason

1. A hazard for a critic who has been at the trade as long as I is that it becomes increasingly difficult consciously to remember all that has influenced me. In this and the following chapter I try to indicate what I believe are my primary critical debts, but I am surely overlooking some commentaries whose effect on my thinking will be apparent to others—for which I can only offer this general apology.

2. Wordsworth and Coleridge were the most significant models to be challenged for the younger romantics, but today we undoubtedly underestimate the importance of what we call "minor" poets such as Scott and Southey, who also offered interesting target models for Byron, Shelley, and Keats. Because economic and social changes, even changes in publishing, were creating new conceptions of the functions of "literature" and of literary artists, popular and publicly notable writers were then unusually influential in ways that our criticism has yet to assess fully. Among commentaries in this area, G. Kim Blank's *Wordsworth's Influence on Shelley* (New York: St. Martin's, 1988) is indispensable; and Beth Lau's *Keats's Reading of the Romantic Poets* (Ann Arbor: University of Michigan Press, 1991) is helpful in its systematic presentation of citations.

7. refiguring reason

3. "The Fall of Hyperion: A Dream," canto 1, lines 16–18, in *The Poems of John Keats*, ed. Jack Stillinger (Cambridge, Mass.: Harvard University Press, 1978), 478. All my citations of Keats's poetry are from this edition.

4. Among the numerous studies of the "Hyperion" poems to which I know I am indebted, I mention first Stuart Sperry's still-indispensable *Keats the Poet* (Princeton: Princeton University Press, 1973), because this remains among the most judicious and helpful commentaries. Claude Finney's *The Evolution of Keats's Poetry* (New York: Russell and Russell, 1963) continues to be valuable for its detailed descriptions of Keats's artistic development, as does even Maurice Ridley, *Keats's Craftsmanship* (Oxford: Clarendon, 1933). John Bayley's "Keats and Reality," in *Proceedings of the British Academy* (London: Oxford University Press, 1962), 91–125, and Christopher Ricks's *Keats and Embarrassment* (Oxford: Clarendon, 1974) are valuable, stimulating studies. Ian Jack, *Keats and the Mirror of Art* (Oxford: Clarendon, 1967) remains unsuperseded as a general discussion of its topic, which has considerable relevance for the "Hyperion" poems. The principal biographies of Keats, Walter Jackson Bate, *John Keats* (Cambridge, Mass.: Harvard University Press, 1963), and Aileen Ward, *John Keats: The Making of a Poet* (New York: Viking, 1963), are particularly useful on the "Hyperion" poems, and of course Hermione de Almeida, *Romantic Medicine and John Keats* (New York: Oxford University Press, 1991), as I have already indicated, by extending and elaborating the valuable work of Donald C. Goellnicht. *The Poet-Physician: Keats and Medical Science* (Pittsburgh: University of Pittsburgh Press, 1984) has provided a perspective on these works that will influence the direction of Keatsian studies for years to come. I should mention two works whose approaches I have found interestingly contrastive with my own angle on Keats: Alan Bewell, "The Political Implications of Keats's Classicist Aesthetics," *Studies in Romanticism* 25 (1986): 220–29; and David P. Haney, "Viewing 'the Viewless Wings of Poesy': Gadamer, Keats, and Historicity," *Clio: A Journal of Literature, History, and the Philosophy of History* 18 (1989): 103–22. For many years I have found the annotations in Miriam Allott, *The Poetry of John Keats* (London: Longmans, 1970), extraordinarily helpful in both their accuracy and their comprehensiveness.

5. I introduce D. W. Winnicott's psychological theories, my chief reference here being his *Playing and Reality* (New York: Basic Books, 1971), 106–10, in part because his admitted and often apparent debt to romantic poets such as Wordsworth (in the present case, the celebrated "Blest be the infant babe" passage from the *Prelude* leaps to mind) suggests that their proto-ecological tendencies may have had more direct influence than is easily recognized.

6. I cite the translation provided by Thomas McFarland in his *Romanticism and the Forms of Ruin* (Princeton: Princeton University Press, 1981), 375. The original may be found in Arthur Schopenhauer, *Sämtliche Werke*, 3d ed., ed. Arthur Hübscher, 7 vols. (Wiesbaden: F. A. Brockhaus, 1972), vol. 3, 404–5.

7. Consult Anne K. Mellor, "Keats's Face of Moneta: Sources and Meaning," *Keats-Shelley Journal* 25 (1976): 65–80, especially 78, for a cogent discussion of this potent image.

8. This point has been admirably articulated by P.M.S. Dawson in " 'The Mask of Darkness': Metaphor, Myth, and History in Shelley's 'The Triumph of Life,' " in *History and Myth: Essays on English Romantic Literature*, ed. Stephen C. Behrendt (Detroit: Wayne State University Press, 1990), 235–42, an essay to which my comments on "The Triumph" are profoundly indebted—as they are to Dawson's earlier fine book on Shelley, *The Unacknowledged Legislator* (Oxford: Clarendon, 1980). I have in my first chapter indicated my admiration for Tilottima Rajan's chapter on "The Triumph" in her *Supplement of Reading: Figures of Understanding in Romantic Theory and Practice* (Ithaca: Cornell University Press, 1990), particularly her success at going beyond Paul de Man's "Shelley Disfigured" in *Deconstruction and Criticism*, ed. Harold Bloom (New York: Continuum, 1979). Rajan's formalism, however, needs to be supplemented by Dawson's mastery of the historical context of Shelley's art as well as the precision of his detailed readings. In less direct ways my understanding of "The Triumph" (and other of Shelley's poems discussed in the next chapter) have indubitably been influenced by several of the excellent monographs that have appeared in the last five years, among which Jerrold E. Hogle's *Shelley Process: Radical Transference and the Development of His Major Works* (New York: Oxford University Press, 1988) is perhaps the most impressive, although Stephen C. Behrendt, *Shelley and His Audiences* (Lincoln: University of Nebraska Press, 1989), Timothy Clark, *Embodying Revolution: The Figure of the Poet in Shelley* (Oxford: Clarendon, 1989), and Christine Gallant, *Shelley's Ambivalence* (New York, St. Martin's, 1989) all make substantial contributions. The analysis of "The Triumph of Life" in Stuart Sperry's *Shelley's Major Verse: The Narrative and Dramatic Poetry* (Cambridge, Mass.: Harvard University Press, 1988) has helped to clarify my thinking about the poem, even though, as I indicate in the next chapter, there are significant divergences between our readings of Shelley.

9. "The Triumph of Life," lines 1–20, in *Shelley's Poetry and Prose*, ed. Donald H. Reiman and Sharon B. Powers (New York: Norton, 1977), 455. All my citations of Shelley's prose and poetry in this chapter and the next are from this edition.

10. P.M.S. Dawson, " 'The Mask of Darkness': Metaphor, Myth, and History in Shelley's 'The Triumph of Life,' " 242–43.

11. Ibid., 241–42. A cogent if dense explanation of why Venus may be both morning and evening "star," although for millennia the planet was described as two different "stars," is to be found in Thomas S. Kuhn, *The Copernican Revolution* (Cambridge, Mass.: Harvard University Press, 1957), 49. The apparently abstruse point is important, because (as many commentators have noted) Venus plays a significant role in Shelley's poetry and does so because Shelley seems to have understood why the complexity of planetary motions were crucial to launching the Copernican revolution of Ptolemaic astronomy (see Kuhn's chapter "The Problem of the Planets," 45–67).

12. Shelley's representation of Rousseau's imaginative limitations, shrewdly analyzed by Edward Duffy in *Rousseau in England* (Berkeley and Los Angeles: University of California Press, 1979), neatly summed up on p. 132, dramatizes the essence of English romantic poetry's critique of the Enlightenment as articulated by Wordsworth—a brilliant discussion of which will be found in Margery Sabin's *English Romanticism and the French Tradition* (Cambridge, Mass.: Harvard University Press, 1976), especially chap. 4, "The Sources of Imagination." The peculiar value of Sabin's comparative study lies in its establishing the importance to the Wordsworthian romantic tradition of memory as displaying "the freedom of the mind rather than the burden portrayed by Johnson and even by Coleridge" (80). Shelley follows Wordsworth in perceiving memory as a source of "creativity" because capable of self-alteration, not bound to mechanical repetitiousness. As Sabin puts it, "No single meaning of an image is fixed. Like nature itself, the mind is continuously growing and changing, becoming something other than it was without ceasing to be itself" (96). Gerald Edelman's explanation of the neuronal system by which human memory operates, described in my final chapter, is precisely congruent with this radical Wordsworthian-Shelleyan concept of memory as a self-altering skill.

13. The most accessible of these ideas are vividly presented by Stephen Jay Gould in several works, such as *The Panda's Thumb* (New York: Norton, 1980), and *Bully for Brontosaurus* (New York: Norton, 1991). Perhaps the most important modification of Darwin's original enunciation proposed by scientists of Gould's persuasion lies in the rejection of simple gradualism, the recognition that sometimes evolution operates through abrupt, seemingly arbitrary leaps. "Evolution, Gould observes in *Bully for Brontosaurus*, for example, "is continual change, but not insensibly gradual transition; in any continuum, some positions are always more interesting than others" (56). This idea of evolution as "punctuated equilibrium" fits rather well not only with Larmarckian emphasis upon the effects of individual change but also with Cuvier's and other such paleontologists' conception of the earth's history as marked by abrupt "catastrophes." On Erasmus Darwin and his influence one should consult Desmond King-Hele, *Doctor of Revolution: The Life and Genius of Erasmus Darwin* (London: Faber and Faber, 1977); and *Erasmus Darwin and the Romantic Poets* (New York: St. Martin's, 1986).

14. G. Kim Blank describes this fluid quality admirably: "Shelley cannot, in composing poetry, hold or sustain a single image before it fades away or becomes another image. His poetry is, to borrow and extend just a part of one of Wordsworth's most famous phrases, the spontaneous overflow of powerful images, one overflowing into another" (*Wordsworth's Influence on Shelley*, 16).

15. Edward Duffy's reading of "The Triumph," 106–52, is particularly illuminating on Shelley's use of "holistically integrative" language.

16. Sperry's discussion of the poem's title, on p. 193, is splendid.

17. The character and significance of the shift in Byron's relation to his reading public, signaled by his change of publishers for *Don Juan*, has been most incisively demon-

strated by William St. Clair, "The Impact of Byron's Writings: An Evaluative Approach," in *Byron: Augustan and Romantic*, ed. Andrew Rutherford (London: Macmillan, 1990), 1–25. This is a truly important essay, which demonstrates persuasively that Byron's original audience, consisting largely of noblemen and affluent gentlemen and their ladies, fell away as they realized that the poet did not in fact share their views, whereas in the 1820s Byron gained a new readership consisting largely of the educated lower middle and upper working classes. Because St. Clair's most telling evidence is of the popularity of piracies of Byron's later work, it is noteworthy that Byron's publisher's fruitless effort to protect his copyright of *Cain* was provoked by a piracy of the drama—the lord chancellor ruling the drama could not be protected by copyright because it was blasphemous. Steffan (see n. 19) provides an admirable summary of this highly revealing legal comedy (13–15).

18. On the origins and spread of "higher criticism" into England one may consult with profit E. S. Shaffer, *"Kubla Khan" and The Fall of Jerusalem: The Mythological School in Biblical Criticism and Secular Literature, 1770–1880* (Cambridge: Cambridge University Press, 1975).

19. My references to *Cain* derive from the text in *Lord Byron's Cain*, ed. and annotated by Truman Guy Steffan (Austin: University of Texas Press, 1968), still indispensable not only for its textual annotations but for its essays on many aspects of the play (for instance, the legal battles surrounding it referred to above in n. 17) and its critical history. By far the most comprehensive recent commentary on Byron's drama is that of Ricardo J. Quinones in *Changes of Cain* (Princeton: Princeton University Press, 1991), 87–108, especially valuable for definition of Byron's innovation upon the most important Enlightenment version of the Cain story, Gessner's *The Death of Abel*. This chapter significantly enlarges Quinones's earlier essay on the topic and is exceptionally helpful in the judiciousness with which it situates Byron's drama in literary history, demonstrating how Byron radically reoriented the Cain story in fashion whose influence continues into our own times. Also useful is the volume *Byron, the Bible, and Religion*, ed. Wolf Z. Hirst (Newark: University of Delaware Press, 1991), the first four essays of which (including an earlier version of Quinones's chapter) deal exclusively with *Cain*. The chief limitation in most of these valuable critiques to my mind lies in their failure to recognize how profoundly Byron's manipulation of biblical material is determined by his concern with other literary reworkings—most importantly, of course, Milton's *Paradise Lost*. Steffan, to the contrary, is fully aware of how deeply mediated by his interest in the "topical" relevance of Milton is Byron's concern with biblical sources and controversies.

20. Equivalently, Cain, resisting "life that leads to death" (*Cain*, 1.2.19), scorns his father's praise of God for enabling good to spring from evil (2.2.290–305) in a manner that inevitably recalls Adam's exclamation to Michael in *Paradise Lost*: "O goodness infinite, goodness immense! / That all this good of evil shall produce, / And evil turn to good"

(12.469–71). Through Byron's drama there are also repeated allusions to Eve's discussions with the serpent that call into question Milton's representation.

21. Peter L. Thorslev, Jr., "Byron and Bayle: Biblical Skepticism and Romantic Irony," in *Byron, the Bible, and Religion*, 58–76.

22. Sigmund Freud, *Moses and Monotheism*, trans. Katherine Jones (1939; reprint, New York: Vintage, 1969), 102–7, 167–68; the significance of this articulation of Freud's speculation is that he is adamantly reaffirming what he had suggested many years before in *Totem and Taboo*. Freud of course exemplifies the tendency to explain phenomena through appeal to a singular "universal" principle—a tendency antithetical to the romantic preference for explanation productive of ambivalence because centered on "unresolvable" competitions between different, even contradictory, modes of organization or assessment.

8. Shelley: The Socialization of Mind

1. Citations of Shelley's poetry are from *Shelley's Poetry and Prose*, ed. Donald H. Reiman and Sharon B. Powers (New York: Norton, 1977). The most important study of Shelley's relation to Wordsworth, as I have previously observed, is that of G. Kim Blank, *Wordsworth's Influence on Shelley* (New York: St. Martin's, 1988). In n. 7 of chap. 7 I have indicated some of the more valuable recent commentaries on Shelley's thought and art, to which I might add here John A. Hodgson's *Coleridge, Shelley, and Transcendental Inquiry* (Lincoln: University of Nebraska Press, 1989) for an approach quite different from mine. Representative of critical enthusiasm for the "Ode to the West Wind" is Stuart Curran's extended discussion of the poem in his *Shelley's "Annus Mirabilis": The Maturing of an Epic Vision* (San Marino, Calif.: Huntington Library, 1975), 156–72, while Judith Chernaik's analysis in *The Lyrics of Shelley* (Cleveland: Case Western Reserve University Press, 1972) is still well worth consulting.

2. I am increasingly inclined to identify this capacity to conceive of "nature" as self-transformative (which requires continuous questioning of the conventional meaning of "nature") as the source of those accomplishments that distinguish the canonical romantic poets and novelists from their "minor" contemporaries and essayists, among whom Hazlitt may be the most pertinent example. No writer of the period more consistently insists that "poetry is the language of imagination," as he says in "On Poetry in General," and that there "a strength in the imagination that reposes entirely on nature," as he observes in "Why the Arts Are Not Progressive." But Hazlitt's "nature" is a conventionalized abstraction. He does not recognize how differently different people may conceive "nature" or consider that "nature" may be above all else dynamically self-transforming. This is why for him the arts cannot "progress," and he unwittingly arrives at essential agreement with Peacock against Shelley that art in the modern world is imagination exercised trivially. The sturdy changelessness of Hazlitt's politics derives from the same source; contrarily, the anguished complexity, often leading into contradic-

171

tions, of the poets' idealisms is rooted in their more complex ambivalences about "nature."

3. Shelley's comment on "Buffon's sublime but gloomy theory, that this earth which we inhabit will at some future period be changed into a mass of frost" is quoted by P.M.S. Dawson in his splendid essay " 'The Mask of Darkness': Metaphor, Myth, and History in Shelley's 'The Triumph of Life,' " in *History and Myth: Essays on English Romantic Literature*, ed. Stephen C. Behrendt (Detroit: Wayne State University Press, 1990), 235–42, 240.

4. Stephen Jay Gould presents the most cogent articulation I know of why biological evolution is such a bad analogue for cultural change in "The Panda's Thumb of Technology," in *Bully for Brontosaurus* (New York: Norton, 1991), 55–75. The most disastrous effects of that analogue were probably produced by various kinds of "Social Darwinism" in the late nineteenth and early twentieth centuries, but it has continued to confuse thinking about the relations of nature to culture to this day. A major attraction of the "Neural Darwinism" I describe in my final chapter is that it provides a plausible evolutionary explanation for why humankind has achieved capabilities that can supersede purely natural processes—among which perhaps the most important is that of cultural recovery, because, as Gould puts it, other "organisms cannot recruit the virtues of their lost pasts" (62).

5. An impressive demonstration of the "radical" character of Shelley's "philhellenism" is provided by Mark Kipperman, who rightly observes that in 1821 "philhellenism could have been seen as nothing less than a challenge to the global order of empires negotiated in 1815." Mark Kipperman, "Macropolitics of Utopia: Shelley's *Hellas* in Context," in *Macropolitics of Nineteenth-Century Literature*, ed. Jonathan Arac and Harriet Retvo (Philadelphia: University of Pennsylvania Press, 1991), 86–100, 90. The particular value of Kipperman's argument is that it counters the prevalent prejudice that "returns to the past," such as one sees in romantic Hellenism, are inevitably ideologically "reactionary." So far as one can generalize on the matter, the evidence is that appeals to a past not immediate but distant are more frequently aimed at progressive (rather than reactionary) purposes—just as I suggested in the preceding chapter that Keats and Shelley made use of the medieval dream-vision in order to liberate themselves from recent neoclassic formal limitations.

6. The gravest weaknesses in current Wordsworth criticism derive from a failure to recognize how the dynamics of the poet's conception of memory's mutability put him in diametric opposition to traditional ideas of how memory functions. Wordsworth's understanding of memory as changeable, as therefore a "skill," finds validation today in Edelman's research, which I describe in chap. 9. Among the few critics who have grasped the originality of Wordsworth's view of memory, Margery Sabin is the most perceptive. I have already pointed out that in her essential but frequently overlooked book *English Romanticism and the French Tradition* (Cambridge, Mass.: Harvard University Press,

1976) she decisively distinguishes Wordsworth's treatment of memory, observing that he "reinterprets memory to signify the freedom of the mind rather than the burden portrayed by Johnson and even by Coleridge" (80). Later she correctly observes that for Wordsworth, "Images remain alive in the mind, changing and growing. The activity of memory is a new act of imaginative perception. The poetic mind remolds the forms of the past, as it remolds the objects of perception in all acts of vision" (95).

7. "The Defence of Poetry," in *Shelley's Poetry and Prose*, 498.

8. One of the several features of ecological criticism that the hortatory purpose of this introductory study precludes my developing is its potential for allowing us to recognize and evaluate the historical limitations to which all languages (historical phenomena par excellence) are subject. It is not true, as many current critics seem to assume, that anything is easily expressible in any language at any stage in its history. This does not mean than we are justified in regarding any language as generically "primitive" or "sophisticated." Every language of which we know appears equally unlimited in its *capabilities*. Particular efficacies of discourse, however, are not equally available at every point in a given language's history—if they were, languages would be metahistorical phenomena. What has, I think, obscured this simple truth is that language is a tool, and with all tools a single invention or improvement can almost instantly be adapted and put to use in another culture. The ax did not have to be endlessly reinvented. Every human invention offers itself to the service of the entire race. Language is the most valuable of human tools, and every linguistic development presents itself as a potential model to all other languages. The reverse side of the notorious "untranslatability" of languages is the swiftness with which one can assimilate into its own systems functions of another with which it comes in contact. One of the subtlest and most penetrating discussions of such problems inherent to the historicity of language as it affects literary art is that of U. R. Anantha Murthy, "Search for an Identity: A Viewpoint of a Kannada Writer," in *Identity and Adulthood*, ed. Sudhir Kakar (Delhi: Oxford University Press, 1979), 105–17.

9. I am here, of course, following the brilliant analysis of William Keach in his excellent *Shelley's Style* (London: Methuen, 1984), 194–200, which should be read in conjunction with G. Kim Blank's characteristically shrewd commentary in *Wordsworth's Influence on Shelley*. Among the numerous critiques on the poem, besides those in works on Shelley already listed, I would recommend Frances Ferguson, "Shelley's 'Mont Blanc': What the Mountain Said," in *Romanticism and Language*, ed. Arden Reed (Ithaca: Cornell University Press, 1984). Ferguson carries forward a fascination with "sublimity" that has been a dominant feature of romantic criticism for many years. That fascination seems to me another manifestation of the Cold War mentality, particularly in its excluding serious consideration of beauty, which for leading philosophers of the sublime, such as Burke and Kant, was nearly as important as sublimity, and for the English romantic poets usually more important. In Byron's *Cain*, for example, the grandeur of Cain's journey

through cosmic space repeatedly is challenged by his wonder at the beauty of celestial objects, and he ultimately evaluates the entire journey as inferior to the beauty of his sister-wife Adah—to the displeasure of Lucifer, whose liking for the masculinely sexist Burkeian sublime fits snugly into his ethic of abstract universalizing, his desire to separate intellectuality from sensory experience.

10. "Hymn before Sunrise," lines 3–15, in *The Poems of Samuel Taylor Coleridge*, ed. E. H. Coleridge (London: Oxford University Press, 1912), 376–80. A useful introduction to the contrast I am emphasizing will be found in Adam J. Frish, "Contrasting Styles: Teaching 'Mont Blanc' with Coleridge's 'Hymn before Sunrise,' " in *Approaches to Teaching Shelley's Poetry*, ed. Spencer Hall (New York: Modern Language Association, 1990), 59–61, along with the essay in the same volume by Leon Waldoff, "Wordsworth and the Shelleyan Self," 127–31, which is especially good on the parallels and differences in the two poets' representations of power.

11. Valuable for an understanding of the functions of silence in Shelley's art is the essay of John B. Pierce, " 'Mont Blanc' and *Prometheus Unbound*: The Rhetoric of Silence," *Keats-Shelley Journal* 38 (1989): 103–26.

12. Stuart Curran provides a good account of the intertwined composition of the two dramas in his *Shelley's "Annus Mirabilis"* as well as a valuable comparison between them (see esp. 120–30) and offers a germane and important later essay, "The Political Prometheus," *Studies in Romanticism* 25 (1986): 429–55. The books I have cited here and in the preceding chapter by Dawson, Rajan, and Hogle all present extensive analyses of *Prometheus*, and Stuart Sperry gives that play two significant chapters. Commentaries on *The Cenci* are not so rich, but Curran's thorough book on the play, *Scorpions Ringed with Fire* (Princeton: Princeton University Press, 1970), is comprehensive and full of valuable insights.

Barbara Charlesworth Gelpi's *Shelley's Goddess: Maternity, Subjectivity* (New York: Oxford University Press, 1992) is the recent book most relevant to my line of argument, especially in its extended and careful analyses of *Prometheus Unbound*. That Gelpi virtually ignores *The Cenci* and "The Triumph of Life" may suggest the differences between our somewhat parallel approaches. One could pursue the distinction by pointing out that whereas the psychologists most relevant to my thinking are Klein and Winnicott, Gelpi is a devout Freudian-Lacanian, even a Marcusian, to the point of accepting the idea of a "universal incest taboo." Gelpi's view of subjectivity, therefore, is as an "alienated" condition, whereas I see Shelley (like other romantics) striving for participative individuality, understanding subjectivity as a mode of relationship, fulfilled only in reciprocal interactions with an environment. Our divergence is concretized in our reading of the role of earth in *Prometheus Unbound*. I emphasize earth's importance as natural environment; Gelpi concentrates on earth's female gender. I certainly understand why she wishes so to insist, but she runs the risk of producing a mirror inversion of masculinist conceptions and of obscuring the fashion in which romantic poets in testing received conceptions of "nature" inevitably modified traditional assumptions of earth as mother, even as they affirmed earth's maternal function.

13. Gaston Bachelard, the distinguished historian and philosopher of science who in his later career turned to the study of poetry to develop "a complete theory of the imagination," in *L'Air et les songes: Essai sur l'imagination du mouvement* (Paris: Corti, 1943) offers an extended discussion of *Prometheus Unbound* deriving from Shelley's observation in his preface that much of his imagery is "drawn from the operations of the human mind, or from those external actions by which they are expressed" (133). Bachelard's observations include a commentary on lines 89–91 of act 4 congruent with that I have offered on the imagery of "The Triumph of Life": Whence come ye so wild and so fleet, / For sandals of lightning are on your feet / And your wings are soft and swift as thought, . . ." For Bachelard, Shelley's imagery is significantly representative because it is to be understood not symbolically but "as a movement of the imagination," and any "truly poetic image will have something about it that makes it resemble a mental operation." I cite here the translation of Mary McAllester Jones in her valuable essay "On Science, Poetry, and 'the Honey of Being': Bachelard's Shelley," in *Philosphers' Poets*, ed. David Wood (London: Routledge: 1990), 153–76, 171. An adequate translation of Bachelard's entire book is available: *Air and Dreams: An Essay on the Imagination of Movement*, trans. Edith Farrell and C. Frederic Farrell (Dallas: Dallas Institute of Humanities and Culture Publications, 1989).

14. It will be apparent to specialists that, like all recent commentators on *Prometheus Unbound*, my understanding of the play is indebted to the extensive and consistently judicious analysis of Stuart Sperry, *Shelley's Major Verse: The Narrative and Dramatic Poetry* (Cambridge, Mass.: Harvard University Press, 1988), 65–126. Sperry's views in some important respects parallel mine—for example, his perception that "*Prometheus* runs counter to the main current of nineteenth-century literature most of all in its refusal to grant a permanent and unchanging reality to human nature" (113). We diverge principally because of my focus on the ecological. Sperry thinks Shelley saw the "course of evolution had gone terribly wrong" (122), whereas I think that for Shelley, as for contemporary scientists, there was no question of a "right" or "wrong" path for evolution, only the question of appropriate or inappropriate human responses to natural processes. Analogously, I concur with Sperry's insistence on "the ambivalence at the root of the Promethean situation" (75), but I find less puzzling than he Prometheus's combining defiance with forgiveness, his linking the power to endure pain and the power to love, because I do not, like Sperry, read Jupiter as "the father" (80) and Prometheus as the Oedipal son (81). In Shelley's play Jupiter derives his power from Prometheus, not the other way around. This is why the course of Prometheus's development is the opposite of Beatrice's in *The Cenci*. She begins as innocent victim of a parent who then takes on characteristics of her father, whereas Prometheus gives up "Jupiterian" characteristics to become the reverse of Count Cenci and so a redemptive parent rather than a tragic child.

15. Sperry calls attention to Shelley's long-standing attraction to this image, which here finds its culminating expression in his poetry (*Shelley's Major Verse*, 94). One notices that the crux of the comparison lies in its focus on the apparently trivial action that releases tremendous forces, which, I have argued, is also a phenomenon to which Shelley persistently returns.

16. I cite my classroom experience as both a parallel and a contrast to those reported by Stuart Curran, "Shelley's Grasp upon the Actual," in *Approaches to Teaching Shelley's Poetry*, ed. Spencer Hall, 28–31. Although our readings of *The Cenci* differ, Curran and I seem equally determined to upset some traditional conceptions of Shelley's purposes by encouraging our students to evaluate his idealism in terms of his acute perceptions into actual driving forces in human relationships.

17. Here I part company with Sperry, who finds the decisive event in the drama the ironic arrival of the pope's representative to arrest Count Cenci just after he has been murdered (*Shelley's Major Verse*, 132ff.). In my view Robert F. Whitman many years ago stated with splendid precision the tragic crux of the play: "If Beatrice is admirable, it is in spite of, not because of, her act of rebellion. By taking what she thought to be the law of God into her own hands, she acted as a brave and desperate human being—but she was wrong." "Beatrice's 'Pernicious Mistake' in *The Cenci*," *PMLA* 74 (1959): 253. It is worth adding that whether or not protagonists of tragedies are "flawed," figures such as Oedipus, Pentheus, Lear, and Othello indubitably make moral mistakes—as does Beatrice. That critics are reluctant to grant her equivalence to such predecessors may be due in part to her gender; it is difficult to think of a heroine before Beatrice who can sustain such a comparison. Those who sentimentalize Beatrice into victim or noble existentialist obscure the originality of Shelley's attempt to create a genuinely tragic *heroine*, thereby contributing to conventional views that have silenced Beatrice by keeping *The Cenci* off the stage, even though it is not easy to name another drama that so brilliantly displays the destructiveness of patriarchal tyranny.

9. Biology of Mind and the Future of Criticism

1. My sketch of Bachelard's views derives from Mary McAllester Jones's valuable essay "On Science, Poetry, and 'the honey of being,' " in *Philosphers' Poets*, ed. David Wood (London: Routledge, 1990), 153–76, especially 156 and 160. Jones emphasizes how Bachelard's thinking is essential to his argument that we can know more than our own minds, that "consciousness for Bachelard is consciousness of something outside itself" (159). Her analysis reveals how Bachelard's lack of knowledge of the physical functioning of brain structures led him toward defining imagining and reasoning in terms of resistance to outside reality, rather than the more complex interactiveness that Shelley envisioned and Gerald M. Edelman describes.

2. All three of Edelman's books that I cite were published in New York by Basic Books: *Neural Darwinism* in 1987, *The Remembered Present* in 1989, and *Bright Air, Bril-*

liant Fire in 1992. In this last, Edelman analyzes (94–95) the validity of Crick's objections, and in a long "Critical Postscript" to the volume he discusses various criticisms of his work, especially those posed by scholars committed to the brain-computer analogy. For an enthusiastic survey of work along this line in "artificial life," one may consult Steven Levy, *Artificial Life: The Quest for a New Creation* (New York: Pantheon, 1992), which contains some references to recent developments in artificial intelligence studies.

For what little it may be worth, my sense of the crux of the dissatisfaction with Edelman's position by artificial intelligence and artificial life scholars is revealed in a remark of the father of modern computing, John von Neumann: "I shudder at the thought that highly purposive organizational elements, like the protein, should originate in a random process" (*Artificial Life*, 15). The Darwinian idea of evolution that is the basis of Edelman's work, however, accepts chance as an important feature of life processes. Edelman's critics, moreover, have not yet effectively addressed what in *Bright Air, Brilliant Fire* he calls the principle of his search: "There must be ways to put the mind back into nature that are concordant with how it got there in the first place" (15), by which he tries to develop "a biologically based epistemology—an account of how we know and how we are aware in the light of the facts of evolution and developmental biology" (252).

3. Another attractive, and exceedingly interesting, feature of Edelman's work is that it appears congruent with some fundamental psychoanalytic concepts; as Edelman points out in *The Remembered Present*, phenomena such as repression are explicable in terms of his Theory of Neuronal Group Selection (209–12). Arnold Modell, a psychoanalyst at Harvard, has already made use of Edelman's work in *Other Times, Other Realities* (1990) and *The Private Self* (1993), both published by Harvard University Press, as is Merlin Donald's *Origins of the Modern Mind* (1991), a fine study of the development in the past decade of what he calls "mental materialism."

4. One of the most interesting features of Edelman's description of mental development for a humanist—at least for one interested in romantic poetry—is his suggestion of how each infant, within its general physiological capabilities, builds up its own individual world on the basis of what Edelman calls categorization on values, these being experienced internally as feelings. Upon the development and education of feelings, as the romantics steadfastly proclaimed, depends the fullest realization of individualized humanness.

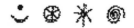

index

index

Ecosystems, 12, 54–60, 73
Edelman, Gerald M., 20, 35, 169n12,
  176n2; and Neural Darwinism,
  142–53; and population thinking,
  157n20
Eliot, T. S., 41, 71
Emotion, in romantic poetry, 5, 7, 52,
  154, 177n4
Environmental historicism, 24, 42, 160n7
Evolution: and chance, 24, 158n3,
  177n2; Darwinian, 23, 90; in "Fall of
  Hyperion, 101–3; Lamarckian, 14, 23;
  90–92, 112; and "punctuated equilibrium," 166n11, 169n13; and romantic
  aesthetics, 89–92, 111–12, 142; Spinoza, and, 60–61
Extinction, concept of, 158n3

Feminism: and ecological criticsm, 6–8;
  and modern biology, 32–36
Ferguson, Frances, 173–74n9
Feynman, Richard, 159n11
Finney, Claude Lee, 167n4
Forster, E. M., 36, 160n16
Frankenstein, and modern science, 28–30
French Revolution, 39, 41–42, 165n3
Frish, Adam J., 174n10
Freud, Sigmund: primal patricide, 118,
  156n8; universal principles in, 171n22
Fryer, Peter, 165n7

Gallant, Christine, 168n8
Gelpi, Barbara Charlesworth, 174–75n12
Genetic engineering, 139, 142
Genetics, "central dogma" of, 32–34
Geology in romantic thought, 165n10
Gilligan, Carol, 156n14
Glacken, Clarence, 26, 159n7

Godwin, William, attacked by Malthus,
  84–87
Goellnicht, Donald C., 157–58n24,
  167n4
Gould, Stephen Jay, 166n11, 169n13,
  172n4
Grabo, Carl, 157n23

Haeckel, Ernst, 22–23, 27, 158n2
Hagleman, Charles W., Jr., 157–58n24
Hampshire, Stuart, 59, 162n7
Haney, David P., 167n4
Hartman, Geoffrey, 37, 68, 162n10,
  163n1
Hazlitt, William, 92, 171–72n2
Heidegger, Martin, 162n3
Heinzelman, Kurt, 164n8
Heisenberg, uncertainy principle, 29–30
Hellenism, romantic, 123–24, 172n5
Herschel, William, 90
Historical tradition and discontinuity,
  123–24
Hodgson, John A., 171n1
Hogle, Jerrold E., 168n8
Holism, 1, 14, 32, 35; and ecology, 19,
  26
Homans, Margaret, 162n10
Hunt, Leigh, 92

Imagination: and consciousness, 138;
  dependent on naturalism, 102–3, 110;
  and evolution, 154; globalizing,
  140–41; and nature, 58, 78–81; refigur-
  ing reality, 107–13; and science, 16–20,
  140
Individuality: and consciousness, 150–51;
  and ecosystem, 106; and feeling, 177n4;
  and holism, 1, 14, 32, 35; masculinist

181

Designer: Linda Secondari
Text: 11/13 Adobe Garamond
Compositor: Columbia University Press
Printer: Maple Vail Manufacturing Group
Binder: Maple Vail Manufacturing Group